W9-CTH-911

HELL IS FOR REAL, TOO

SKIP HUSSEIN SHMULEY was born in Topeka, Kansas, during a tornado at 4:20 p.m. on April 20, 1969, the son of a pawn shop owner and an amateur ballroom dancer. Like so many young men growing up in the 1970s, he dreamed of one day becoming an accountant. In the words of his eleventh grade guidance counselor, "Young Shmuley has a burning desire to change the world, one spreadsheet at a time."

Shmuley got his accounting degree from Cornell in 1991, and finally passed his CPA exam in 2008. He and his current wife and family live in Barstow, California, where the average July temperature is "hotter than hell."

Since his return from hell and the publication of this book, he's been traveling across the United States on the raving lunatic circuit, preaching about the coming apocalypse with the help of a homemade sandwich board. He's also enjoying the freedom that comes from postvasectomy sex and postvasectomy masturbation.

In his spare time, after having a restraining order overturned, he coaches the high school girls' lacrosse team.

His other hobbies include competitive eating and being cuckolded by his wife.

Praise for Skip Shmuley and *Hell Is for Real, Too*

"Skip Shmuley takes the reader deep into the bowels of hell, sloshes them around, and craps them back out again."
　　　　　　　　　　　　　　　　　　　　—Mark Twain

"The lamestream media hate this book, so I love it!"
—Sarah Palin

"Loved it. A tour de force!"   —Charles Manson

"I think this will make a great Pixar movie."
—Hosni Mubarak

"Love the book and admire the man. I checked him out thoroughly."   —John McCain

"Reading what lies in store was enough to change my life around."   —Hugo Chávez

"Hell is heinous."   —Keanu Reeves

"I want more money."   —Jose Reyes

"If you read just one phony, made-up book about religion all year, read *Heaven Is for Real*. If you read two, try this one."   —The Vatican

"Don't steal this book; it's not worth it."
—Abbie Hoffman

"Shall I compare this to a burning bag of doggie doo?"
—William Shakespeare

"Dibs on the movie rights!"   —Leni Riefenstahl

"A fatwa against Mr. Shmuley."

—Mahmoud Ahmadinejad

"There is a hell. Oy vey." —Osama bin Laden

"If hell is the punishment for making people suffer, I am so sorry I made Alabama." —God

"Shmuley's vision of hell is worse than even what I have seen." —Jenna Jameson's gynecologist

"I think I could play the lead when it comes to dinner theater." —Don Knotts

"Hell is much worse than being seated next to me."

—The crying baby in seat 17C

SKIP SHMULEY

~

*A Middle-Aged Accountant's
Astounding Story of
His Trip to Hell
and Back*

~

Hell Is for Real, Too

Illustrations by Leif Parsons

A PLUME BOOK

PLUME
Published by Penguin Group
Penguin Group (USA) Inc., 375 Hudson Street, New York, New York
10014, U.S.A. • Penguin Group (Canada), 90 Eglinton Avenue East, Suite
700, Toronto, Ontario, Canada M4P 2Y3 (a division of Pearson Penguin
Canada Inc.) • Penguin Books Ltd., 80 Strand, London WC2R 0RL, En-
gland • Penguin Ireland, 25 St. Stephen's Green, Dublin 2, Ireland (a div-
ision of Penguin Books Ltd.) • Penguin Group (Australia), 250 Camberwell
Road, Camberwell, Victoria 3124, Australia (a division of Pearson Australia
Group Pty. Ltd.) • Penguin Books India Pvt. Ltd., 11 Community Centre,
Panchsheel Park, New Delhi – 110 017, India • Penguin Books (NZ), 67
Apollo Drive, Rosedale, Auckland 0632, New Zealand (a division of Pearson
New Zealand Ltd.) • Penguin Books (South Africa) (Pty.) Ltd., 24 Sturdee
Avenue, Rosebank, Johannesburg 2196, South Africa

Penguin Books Ltd., Registered Offices: 80 Strand, London WC2R 0RL,
England

First published by Plume, a member of Penguin Group (USA) Inc.

First Printing, November 2011
10 9 8 7 6 5 4 3 2 1

Ⓟ REGISTERED TRADEMARK—MARCA REGISTRADA

LIBRARY OF CONGRESS CATALOGING-IN-PUBLICATION DATA

Shmuley, Skip.
   Hell is for real, too : a middle-aged accountant's astounding story of his trip
to Hell and back / Skip Shmuley.
     p. cm.
   ISBN 978-0-452-29779-1
   1. American wit and humor.   2. Hell—Humor.   3. Devil—Humor.
I. Title.
   PN6165.S49 2011
   808.8'0382023—dc23

                                                        2011032125

Printed in the United States of America
Set in ITC Galliard

To the almighty Supreme Being,
who watches over all of us and determines
our fate and destiny.

By that I mean either Satan or God.

Contents

Acknowledgments

There are so few people to thank who made this book a reality. This book would not have been written if my Dad had worn a condom. So thanks, Mom and Dad; it's amazing what a night of Riunite on ice can lead to.

Next to David Rosenthal and everyone at Plume: you've always been inspiring and encouraging, helping me in every way as I went about sharing the tale of my journey. And to my current wife and kids, the single most sarcastic thanks imaginable, as they were completely not helpful and incredibly antagonistic about this whole venture until they realized I was getting paid and that when I die and don't come back, they will share in the cash. So they think.

To JM, DM, SM, RM, and JK, you know who you are . . . you are those odd people who prefer initials.

And finally to my Scoutmaster Mr. Giffords, who really helped shape my worldview and taught me that what happens in a tent stays in a tent. Or to quote him verbatim, "Boychik, what happens in Resica Falls campground stays at Resica Falls campground." Which was true until the moment when my trip to hell triggered my repressed memory syndrome. Who knew there wasn't a merit badge for testicle tickling? Well now the world knows.

Hell Is for Real, Too

Prologue

In April 1966 *Time* magazine raised the question: "Is God Dead?"

In April 2011 *Time* asked: "What If There Is No Hell?"

I can't answer the former . . . but I can attest to you that hell is in fact very, very real.

I know.

I was there for a long weekend.

This is my story.

ħell Is for Real

All the world knows the amazing story of little Colton Burpo, who nearly died during an emergency appendectomy and then, while in a coma on the operating table, went to heaven. His father's book *Heaven Is for Real* has sold over a million copies and deservedly so. Only a cynic would believe that an evangelical pastor whose son had heard fifty-two thousand Bible stories from him over the years would then, after realizing the family owed thousands in medical bills, do the following: (1) prompt the young lad with leading questions; (2) elicit a story about Jesus, angels, and a God who is "really really big";

(3) write a book with a professional author; and (4) make big bucks off of it.

Heaven . . . and hell forbid that would ever happen.

It is only the nonbelievers and jaded agnostics who doubt good men of the book and cloth like Pastor Ted "Meth and Men" Haggard; Reverend Jimmy "Come Blow Gabriel's Trumpet" Swaggart; Reverend Jim "Shake Your Booty" Bakker; Reverend Eddie "Drop Your Pants, Lad, and Let Me See Your Key to Heaven" Long; and, of course, Terry "Burn, Baby, Burn" Jones. These men are so honest and decent that God himself has ensured they live the lavish lifestyles they so richly deserve. As it is written in Celestines 1:27:

> Thus saith the Lord, he who spreadeth the word of the good book needeth only followeth three of the ten commandments for it is yea my belief that .300 gets you into heaven or the Hall of Fame.

But this is my story, not the Burpos'—and it is as real to me as the story Todd claims Colton told him. And I would swear with my hand on the Holy Bible and say, "If I'm lying send me straight to hell"—but as you will see, I've already been there.

~

Final Four weekend calls up memories of classic basketball games, drinking beer, eating chips, and spending hours in a sports bar watching games with friends. But the Final Four weekend of 2010 was a big deal for other reasons.

It was a Friday afternoon. April 2010. Like a lot of guys, I scheduled my vasectomy to coincide with the NCAA Tournament. My wife and I had decided after Little Timmy that we'd had enough. Personally, I was feeling financially strapped, with eight kids between two different wives and one paternity suit still being adjudicated by Maury; plus, the current wife had been foaling out a kid every few years, so we agreed that spring 2010 was the perfect time to get the old tubes tied. The plan was foolproof. Get snipped on a Friday, lie in bed Saturday through Monday night, embedded in ice, and back to work at my accounting firm on Tuesday. I couldn't think of a better way to spend three days. Watching basketball and staring at my swollen testicles. The idea was once this was done, like Arnold Schwarzenegger and half the NBA, I'd never have to worry again about wearing a condom.

The vasectomy procedure is outpatient. First they have you come in and pleasure yourself so they can get a "pre-operation sperm count" to compare with your numbers after your tubes are tied. They even give you magazines to help along the way. (I chose *Car and Driver* to start and then finished with *Guns and Ammo*.)

It's always a bit awkward when you hand the specimen cup to the nurse, so for laughs, I gave her a half-eaten

Dannon yogurt left over from lunch. One taste and she knew it wasn't real.

After that it was onto the operating table. They covered me with a sheet and asked if I wanted to be mildly sedated or knocked out. Being a bit of a chicken, I asked for the full knockout. They put the mask over me and within minutes I was out. Or was I? It seemed I was trapped in a half-conscious nightmare. I could hear the "snip snip" of the doctor's Dura Shears and the comments of the nurse over the size of my organ. She was really not impressed. I could feel the tugging as they tied me up. And then I was wheeled into the recovery room.

That's when the problems started.

Maybe it's due to health care reform; maybe it's because my urologist is an illegal immigrant running a clinic in his basement. It doesn't matter. What does matter is that within minutes my balls began to swell up like Miss Iowa four years after she wins the crown. I could feel my fever spiking and soon I heard one of the nurses saying, "We're losing him . . . eh." Turns out they're illegal immigrants from Canada.

At this point my chest went into spasm and I could actually feel myself leaving my body. As I looked down I could see the doctor and two nurses working on me. They were desperately trying to jump-start my heart with a pair of jumper cables. I could feel nothing: either I was dead or my body is just used to nipple clamps.

Then I could hear crying and screaming. My wife had burst into the room. She was hysterical that she hadn't been there to see me die. It had always been her wish. There wasn't a night in the past ten years that didn't go by where I would say, "How can I make you happy?" and she would reply, "Overinsure and then die in front of me." We have a typical marriage.

The real world began receding faster than Prince William's hairline. I was pulling away from my wife faster than I do after sex. Then, suddenly, I saw a tunnel and a light, a brilliant, all-encompassing, warm light. I could see Jesus, with his arm around Muhammad, and Moses and Buddha and Joseph Smith and L. Ron Hubbard, Zeus, the Great Pumpkin, and that Wiccan priestess who works at the Starbucks near my house.

Then Jesus spoke.

In Spanish. (Apparently he's a big fan of Rosetta Stone.)

Jesus looked at me and smiled—I never felt more safe. He was amazing: six foot three, buff, perfect nose, blond hair and blue eyes, just like everyone who lived in the Middle East a couple millennia ago. He raised his hand to give me a blessing. And then he yelled, "Have fun in hell!!!"

The hysterical laughter that erupted from Muhammad, Moses, L. Ron, and the other guys was a sure sign that this was how they spent their days, taunting people with a bait and switch.

As I watched them return to their poker game, the clouds crumbled beneath me. The laughter got fainter and fainter as they vanished from sight and I realized I was hurtling down the Highway to Hell. . . .

Raging at God

During the time my body was on the operating table my soul was going straight to hell. Looking up, I saw everything. My wife laughing and crying at the same time, slurring her words from too many wine coolers, demanding to see—and I'm quoting here—"the head sturgeon."

I could see the doctor trying to calm her down as they both reached for the bottle of sedatives she carried with her twenty-four/seven. I could see the doctor slap my wife to end her hysterics. I flew into a rage: why couldn't I have done that?

9

The doctor told my wife, "We've lost your husband; he's gone."

My wife answered, "But he's got his iPhone, can't we track him?"

As I continued my descent, I saw the final images of life here on earth. The sun. Clouds. Flowers. My wife dry-humping a male nurse in a broom closet.

My heart raced, I couldn't get my breath. Desperation, panic, and frustration washed over me like waves over Osama bin Laden. I was all alone, at the entrance of hell.

All of a sudden, an old man appeared. It was the official greeter of hell. Think of a Walmart greeter only older. His name was Oscar. At first I was in denial. I kept saying to myself: "I can't be dead, I have so many things on my bucket list that I'll never get around to doing on earth. This is just a bad dream and soon I'll wake up, as I do every night, to my wife's cleft palate snoring."

The tip-off that maybe I was dead and in hell was the fact that the room temperature was approaching sixteen thousand degrees; plus, the loudspeakers were playing the entire Taylor Swift discography (which, I have come to realize, is really the same song).

I was getting hot under the collar and, in fact, everywhere else. I directed all my anger at Oscar.

"Why am I here?" I screamed. "How can you do this to me? Isn't this a misunderstanding? Why is it so hot here? Does anyone have some SPF 6000?"

I raged for fifteen minutes straight. I was as apoplectic as Maria Shriver when her maid was five weeks late. Oscar stood there motionless. Then slowly, methodically, he reached his hand up, switched on his Miracle-Ear, and said, "Can you repeat that?"

I continued my tirade. I was abusing this old man like he was an orderly in a Medicaid-funded nursing home. Then I threw him a changeup. Out of nowhere I asked, "Where can I find deodorant?"

He said, "Aisle eight."

I knew it! He *was* an actual Walmart greeter. This is where they all go when they die, which is actually a step up from working at Walmart. At least Satan pays union wages.

I continued to rage at God. I took his name in vain; I used more curse words than a rapper with Tourette's. But each slander against the Lord only sealed my fate. Begging and pleading got me nowhere. Regardless of what I said, Oscar had the same quizzical look that my wife had when I told her about the tradition of oral sex on the wedding night.

Finally Oscar said, "Look, you need to calm down. Would you like me to have a doctor prescribe something for you?"

Being a typical middle-aged American male whose life is spent gobbling Lipitor and Xanax like Tic Tacs, I said, "Yes."

Oscar snapped his fingers and a physician magically appeared. It was Dr. Jack Kevorkian.

It finally dawned on me. I really was dead.

The Five Stages of Dying

Elisabeth Kübler-Ross was right. There are five stages of dying and I had already been through two of them: denial and anger. Before I could move on, I had to deal with the next three.

First was bargaining. I looked upward, where I imagined God to be. I beseeched him. "God, if you get me out of here I promise to be a good man. I promise to follow seventy percent of the Ten Commandments. I will never hack into Anthony Weiner's Twitter account again. I will never use the word 'irregardless' again. And I will give one percent of my income to charity."

No response.

"Two percent."

Nothing.

I realized this was the time to throw deep. I said, "Two point five percent. And off the gross, not the net."

Nothing.

I felt a hand gently touch my shoulder . . . then another touched my ass. One was Oscar's. The other hand was a TSA agent's. Why they need to look for concealed weapons when you're dead is beyond me. I later discovered that TSA agents aren't in hell; they just like to volunteer there, for fun.

Oscar gently told me, "It's too late."

I said, "You mean this is it?"

Oscar said, "No, it's too late in the day. This is Friday and God takes off at noon."

Lazy bastard. So it's more of an "on the seventh day he rested but he takes off early and has long weekends" kind of place. I don't remember that part of Genesis.

I became depressed: that's stage four. Nothing could stop me from crying like a twelve-year-old girl who just had her cell phone taken away.

Kübler-Ross said that this is the stage when one becomes aware that nothing can be done, that it's hopeless, like starting for the Miami Heat in the fourth quarter of a playoff game.

Tears began to flow once again. Which is the worst

thing that can happen in hell because Satan feasts on human tears. And on Del Taco. Which explains the odor.

This leads to Kübler-Ross's final stage, the one you need to reach before you are allowed to move on. This is the stage of acceptance, when you realize that you are in fact dead and there is nothing you can do about it.

Oscar could see from my face that I had finally arrived there.

"Shmuley," he gently told me, "you are ready to meet your new neighbors."

And then he told the TSA agent, "Let go of his ass."

The Rooms of Hell

On the lecture circuit the first question I'm always asked is, "Who and what do you see the minute you get to hell?"

Actually that's the second question. The first is, "Is there sex in hell?" The answer to the first is, "No, but like sex, there is often an unpleasant burning sensation." Regarding the second question, here is an overview of the types of people you'll see as you enter those onyx gates.

Your introduction to the other residents of hell begins once you're done with Oscar the greeter. He takes you to a moving sidewalk. As you step on and begin to motor along, you pass a number of rooms where you can see those warehoused in the "coach section." Yes, hell is like flying on a discount airline or living in India in 1935; there are sections divided by class.

The first residents you'll see are child stars. Hundreds and hundreds of child stars. It's no big deal to them since their lives had become a living hell anyway. There's actually an entire room full of Coreys, Corys, and Coris. Plus, at the end of the room is anyone who ever named their baby after where he or she was conceived: Paris; Dakota; Buick.

That next room in hell is full of parents who ever had a bumper sticker that read, "My child is student of the month." (There are no Asian parents. Yes, it's hard to believe a cold, verbally abusive Tiger Mom can get into heaven and you can't. But you know what? Turns out God doesn't care that your kid plays club soccer; he cares that your kid plays the cello. And is polite. And is better at math than Stephen Hawking. That would be the Stephen Hawking who when he gets to hell will wish he hadn't announced there is no God or heaven. Anyway, compared to the Tiger Mom's kids, all of ours are on the short yellow bus.)

The next room of people in hell is full of snarky men and women writing blogs about hell. Each one desperately trying to sell enough ad space to make a full-time living so they can quit their job at the Verizon store in hell. Which is redundant.

The next room is an odd combination. Half of them are those midlevel city officials—you know the type. The ones who would close down a little girl's lemonade stand because she's operating it without a permit. The other half are the little girls themselves, who flagrantly violate the law and think the rules don't apply to them; those basically weepy little trollops with obese parents who either shoved them into "toddlers and tiaras" beauty pageants or forced them onto the evening news to whine that their lukewarm *E. coli*–filled lemonade stand was shut down. Whatever happened to sleeping with the guy from the Bureau of Licenses to get around the permits? I bet Tiger Mom would have given that bureaucrat a tumble to keep little Brittany's lemonade stand open.

Next is the room reserved for anyone who's ever swirled a glass of wine for more than ten seconds before drinking it. In hell, they're forced to wear an artsy black turtleneck, which grows progressively tighter year after year, cutting off their olfactory senses until they can no longer discern between a five-hundred-dollar cabernet and a bottle of Thunderbird.

Next to that is the special room for people with OCD. This room is unlocked, with a doorway that leads directly to a back stairway out of hell that goes straight into heaven. You're free to leave at any time. Unfortunately no one is willing to touch the doorknob, nor can they get their feet positioned just right on the tiles in the foyer.

Then there are a series of gloomy, miserable solitary confinement cubicles, reserved for anyone who's ever used the phrase, "I just need some 'me' time." So it's for every-one in L.A.

Yet another hellish room is the one full of all the folks who have ever gone to sex rehab. God knows there is no such thing as a sex addict—and Satan knows it, too. In fact, everyone knows it except the therapists who claim it is a real condition. Satan's idea of punishing them for their horny self-pity is to lock them up together, load them with Viagra and ecstasy, and then put them in chastity belts.

Soon you start to hear construction noises. That's the room in hell actually undergoing a remodeling. It has been under construction since the dawn of time. If you were an overachieving go-getter in life who needed things done "yesterday," your fate is to live in this remodel. You'll spend all of eternity being told by contractors "Just two more weeks."

Did you know you could go to hell for tweeting? There's a special group in hell made up entirely of people who post photos of every single meal they eat at a restaurant. If this is you, you'll be stripped naked, hog-tied, and placed on a large platter with an apple in your mouth. You're sur-rounded by six-foot-tall sweet potatoes, pork belly sliders, and red velvet cupcakes that take photos of you all day long while commenting how this dish looks "a-ma-zing."

Then comes a rumpus room of sorts. It's for any-one who has ever called California "the Left Coast" or has consistently used the term "chief," "sport," or "ace" to address total strangers here on earth. They serve their sentence being backslapped by other chiefs, sports, and aces until their vertebrae shatter and their spine falls out of alignment. When they mention the pain, they're henceforth addressed as "total pussy."

The next room is filled with overweight, bald, hairy-chested New York expatriates, you know who I mean. These are the ones who would ruin any Super Bowl party by saying, "You can't get good pizza anywhere but back home." Their room is catered in perpetuity by Little Caesar's.

~

Imagine a giant hall filled with attractive, single young women, each one of whom was struck down in the middle of the road while wandering into the street oblivious of traffic while talking on her cell phone. If you think stretch marks ruin a good twenty-year-old flat belly, try tire marks. The worst part is even now, they're still talking on their cell phones.

The adjacent room has exactly seventy-two people in it. The famous seventy-two virgins, the ones who comfort "martyrs," but it's not what the jihadists had in mind. It's a trap. Those who have access to this room think this is a great deal. Except for one little problem. Remember that fat chick your freshman year at State College, the one you popped after two bottles of Gallo Spanada? Remember how clingy she got for the next four years?

Imagine an eternity in the same room with her. After deflowering, each one of these girls will cling to you as the first love of her life forever. It takes four thousand years to duck out of committing to each one of these girls. And in hell, they can find you . . . Satan gives them your phone number and he's banned caller I.D.

Next door to the seventy-two-virgin room is a room for men only, with great, comfortable chairs and wall-to-wall televisions. All showing *Kathie Lee and Hoda*.

And then there's the room that is empty except for one woman. She lived in L.A., was forty-five years old, and everyone knows why she is there alone except her. Let's just call it "oversharing about her digestive problems."

Next is a room filled with local news anchors. Hundreds of almost-attractive people all grouped by fours: the blow-dried white guy or uptight Asian guy paired with either an African American or Latino anchorwoman, the wacky weather guy, and somebody named Fred doing sports. There are thousands of them sitting at their desks staring straight ahead or slowly turning to camera from a side pose to give you that full frontal shot. They are there for eternity, getting makeup, having fake banter with each other, and rearranging papers on their desks as they wait for the big story that will never come. These are the folks who have never learned that with the Internet, we don't have to wait until eleven p.m. to find out about the local missing trailer park woman.

The next room has the tightest squeeze. It's all the major league baseball players who used steroids. There are only fifteen guys there, but with their giant heads and ridiculous biceps, the room is really crowded.

The room after that doesn't look like it belongs in hell because it is full of gorgeous women. All supermodels. Then you realize why. In a world of hunger and famine, no one appreciates people who choose not to eat. Or even worse, the ones who eat and then purge. Forget purgatory, this is purge-atory.

And then the final room. It is best described as a bad

spa day at the Dead Sea. Millions of Europeans in Speedos. All of them. Imagine a place with commingled sweat, mud, and chest hair coupled with rude French waiters, humorless German comics, and bad English food. That's where hell warehouses those God never wanted in the first place. Remember, God made the world in six days and on the seventh day he rested. That's the day Satan made Europeans.

Some places in Hades are not actually rooms, they're destinations. Really bad destinations. Like taking a departing flight from Camden and landing in Newark. You arrive in the worst heat imaginable. The hair on your body singes off like a three-dollar Brazilian wax at a strip mall. Just as you think you can't take it anymore, you walk outside to a pool. A beautiful, crystal clear infinity pool, overlooking a scenic lagoon. Perfect temperature. There are only five other people in the pool. Their faces aren't clear, but you can tell they are neither ugly nor attractive, not really men or women. Think Chaz Bono. You get in and begin to swim around. It's cleansing, it's refreshing. You begin to think, "If this is hell, then let me sin." Then suddenly you hit a warm spot. Then another, then another. That's right, this is for people who peed in a pool. If this includes you, you better start repenting. What's wrong with these people? Don't they know that even hell has bathrooms? Which leads us to . . .

The Throne Room of Satan

y first Christmas back among the living, I picked a story to read. It was an old fable about two women who live together, each with an infant son. Well, to be honest, it was actually a Facebook page made by two women living together, and I'm pretty sure they both have kids. All right, fine, it was a video about two horny MILFs who both want to bang the handyman. You happy? Anyway, desperate for his affections, the two women practically tear him in half while fighting over him. It reminded me of what they call "the Solomon solution." I think it was because King Solomon once, while sitting on his throne, threatened to split a baby in half, and it turns out this handyman kept yelling, "I'm gonna split you in half, baby!"

My point, and I had one, is that whenever I think about Solomon sitting on his throne, it reminds me of one of the most treacherous places in all of hell, the Throne Room of Satan. It is where Beelzebub does his filthy business while reading the financial page—he likes to see how his minions on Wall Street are doing.

The Throne Room of Satan is right past the door to room 10. As the moving sidewalk ends, there's a gigantic door. It has a sign on it that reads, "Abandon all stomach contents, ye who enter here." And to make sure those who went to public school understand, it has a picture of a stick-figure man doubled over clutching his stomach. No one tells you whether to go in or stand there, so after what seemed like an eternity, I decided to enter. And though I've tried to block it from memory, I'll describe it as best I can.

The Throne Room of Satan . . . imagine an outhouse at a Tijuana cockfight in August. Now imagine while you're in there, some local kids do the old "push it over with the door side on the ground" trick. Now imagine you wait so long for a rescue crew to arrive you're forced to survive on reclaimed tomato skins and corn. Compared to this, that's the Ritz.

For starters, every toilet in the Throne Room of Satan is broken. Ever try getting a plumber to show up in hell?

You know what that costs? And weekends, forget it. The stench is overwhelming. And why bother lighting a match— you're in hell.

Now, Colton Burpo described the throne in heaven as "a chair that only the king can sit in." It's the same way Al Bundy used to describe it on *Married with Children*. From the outside, Satan's personal throne looks like an ordinary stall. It's when you go inside that you realize hell is *really* bad. There's no floor space to lay a newspaper down on, as every square inch of Satan's private throne is filled with the largest ceramic bowl you've ever seen. It's really, really big because Satan is the biggest guy you've ever seen. Think of Mark McGwire the year he hit seventy. And he really, really loves chili, and cabbage, and lasagna with hot peppers. And you wouldn't believe how much he likes bran muffins. Satan could take a dump anywhere he chooses, but he always chooses to go in a large public restroom to inflict as much suffering as possible.

You know how they say cleanliness is next to godliness? Not so much in hell. Coming from the stall beside Satan's, I heard grunting and splashing, then someone cursing in German. At first I thought it was one of those Berlin *Scheisser* videos I've heard so much about. I peeked over the top of the stall, and there was Adolf Hitler. I could see by the veins bulging in his forehead that he was clearly constipated. Or angry. Either way it explains a lot about World War II.

From another stall I heard Arabic. At first I thought I was back on earth at a gas station in Queens. Then I peeked over the top of that stall, and there was Osama bin Laden. Also trying in vain to "purge the demons." Screaming that he wished he had a good Jewish gastroenterologist. Which shocked me. All those lentils and hummus, you'd think he'd get *something*. I mean, Hitler I understand; a diet of bratwurst and schnitzel will bind you up until the end of time.

Now it all began to make sense. Hell isn't about concentric circles; it's about bathroom stalls. The worse you acted in life, the closer you have to shit to the devil and his Mount Vesuvius of an intestinal tract. And you can forget about a courtesy flush. Never. Just the smells of burning phosphate and methane.

As I walked out, I was in a daze from all I'd seen. That's when I met Larry. Larry is the guy who works as a bathroom attendant in the Throne Room of Satan. He has a little setup with mints, candies, and, since it's hell, plenty of Axe body spray and Drakkar Noir. Which is just his excuse to stand by and check out your junk as you're urinating. He learned it from George Michael. The guy just stands there staring; he won't offer you a paper towel because nobody washes their hands in hell, even if they handle food. He's like the WNBA: there, but for what real purpose?

At that moment, the details of my life began to pile up like the stack of Polaroids I used to have before I started filming girlfriends on my camera phone. I thought about how I treated my fellow man back on earth. Was this where I was to end up for eternity, in a shithouse with Hitler reaching under the stall wall asking for the sports section? "How's that Jesse Owens doing?" he'd ask.

I sat down on some cracked porcelain to think and decide what to do next, as my eyes took in what I call the hellholes of hell—the toilets.

Every toilet, and I mean every toilet, is overflowing. And the seats are wet. The newspaper left behind is just the want ads and they're soaked because every flush sends a geyser of water in a random direction. There are only three sheets left on the roll of toilet paper and those aren't Snickers bars floating neat the surface. And it also turns out that not flushing here on earth can land you in hell. Especially if you do it at work.

Naturally, the Throne Room of Satan is covered in graffiti. Every possible rendition of a penis is drawn, carved, or painted on the bathroom walls. It's like the Sistine Chapel of cocks. And like any bathroom, there's plenty of bad-boy boasting and trash talking. "Marie Antoinette gives good head." "Mussolini is a bald fuck!" You have to watch out for the phone numbers—they're as phony as the personals section on Craigslist. And with almost as many serial killers. Ninety percent of them will connect you with a sultry woman, who, with the voice of a young Kathleen Turner, will ask, "Have you considered the extra income an alpaca farm can bring in?"

I WAS TRAMPLED TO DEATH TRYING TO GET THE NEW IPHONE.

REMIND ME NEVER TO GO HUNTING WITH DICK CHENEY AGAIN.

SATAN TAKES CIALIS.

Benedict Arnold IS a squeaker

CLEOPATRA HAS NICE TITS.

ATTILA THE HUN HAS A TINY DICK

8 666 7 530
Jenny

I PLUGGED THIS TOILET FOUR DAYS IN A ROW! - SADDAM

four out of five Devils recommend tridents...

I've Been Sitting here Since 1635 and Still can't pass that leg of Mutton.

WOULD YOU BANG EVA BRAUN?

YES
|||

NO

7 -212-6071
YOUR MOM !

DEPAUL BLUE DEMONS

BLUE DEVILS

ILLINOIS-CHICAGO FLAMES

SUN DEVILS

PALIN/TRUMP 2012

GO RAIDERS !!!

FOR A GOOD TIME 718-223-7349

Why am I down here?
all I did was greenlight
"the Paul Reiser Show."

BLEA BLEA

I LIKE THE NEW "DINNER FOR SCHMUCKS"
BETTER THAN THE ORIGINAL

A guy in a fancy Mercedes
Thought he had a real way with the ladies
Till he gave it a go
With a knife-wielding ho
Now he's scratching his crabs down in Hades

~

There once was a man with no mirth
Who talked about Hell up on Earth
"Hell" didn't mean gloom
Or a fiery doom
But a chick flick starring Colin Firth

~

There once was a priest with a fiddle
Who quizzed everyone with a riddle
"I'll give you one guess
So please try your best:
Which altar boy did I diddle?"

~

There once was a man on vacation
Who was sent to eternal damnation
"I'm down here," he cried
"'Cause the way that I died"—
Autoerotic asphyxiation

~

There once was a man, so I'm told
Who spent fifty years on this bowl
He pushed and he grunted
But his bowels were stunted
By a ten-pound Velveeta cheese roll

Every wall in every stall has a glory hole. Which is a nightmare for those prairie-dogging because it can be tough to relieve yourself when you're being gouged in the side of the head by two incoming schlongs. And whatever you do, don't even think about putting *your* dick in there. It will get stuck and they'll need the Jaws of Life to cut you out as onlookers poke their heads in the stall, take pictures, and laugh. You will then have to repeat this every day for eternity.

As I took all this in, I wondered why I had been allowed into Satan's Throne Room. Was it to meet El Jefe? But Satan wasn't using the throne when I got there. Turns out my meeting with him was just minutes away. . . .

Meeting Satan

I woke up the first morning in hell, in what seemed to be a Motel 6 room . . . except no one had left the lights on. The reason I'm pretty sure it was a Motel 6 is when my eyes got accustomed to the dim light, I saw Tom Bodett sitting in the easy chair. He wasn't saying a word, but then again, he didn't need to. The only thing anyone had ever asked him was, "Are you supposed to be somebody important? Because we can't figure out why Motel 6 put you in their ads."

Anyway, I was famished. As I looked around the room I saw someone had slipped a note under my door. It was when I walked over to get the note that I noticed the light switch. It had a cover and the switch was where Satan's penis would be. I turned on the light and got my first real view of the private rooms in hell. Imagine the low-roller room at Circus Circus, but with the DNA-magnifying black light on the whole time. The entire room looked like a Day-Glo Rorschach test.

The note said, "Breakfast at eight. All you can eat."

Since I was no longer worried about my cholesterol, I went downstairs and walked into the dining room. There was a pretty impressive buffet; I was stunned. But as I approached the line, a large man said, "Mr. Shmuley, have you watched the orientation video? You don't get the free breakfast until you watch the video."

As I was ushered out of the breakfast line I heard two people snickering, "Newbie." After a short walk over burning hot coals, I entered the video screening room. First there was paperwork, then a not-to-scale model of hell to look at. I never knew there was so much to learn. I thought you just died, showed up, and rotted. Even worse, there was a test at the end. "What happens if I flunk the test?" I asked. "What are you going to do? Send me to hell?"

You would think that in six thousand years (since the time the Kentucky Creation Museum said we first lived with dinosaurs) that someone would've asked that just once, but they were stumped. So stumped, in fact, that they had to call in the big guy. Satan himself. My question had raised all kinds of hell.

They took me to a waiting room. It was a lot like my doctor's waiting room. A very pleasant receptionist walked out and told me, "I'm sorry, Satan is going to be a little bit late. She's getting her hair done."

That's right, "she."

There's something you need to know about hell: Satan takes on a different form for everyone. Satan appears as each person's worst nightmare. For some, it could be an IRS agent. For others it's an old boss. For a few it might be John Mayer. For most new entrants, it's the cast of *The View* naked. For me it was different. Satan walked in the room and I said, "Hello, Susan." It was my first wife. Although she was still alive on earth, at least from the waist up, Satan had manifested itself in her image to strike fear in my heart.

After shaking her tail, Satan said to me, "Are there any questions you want to ask?"

I said, "What time's lunch?"

Satan said, "I was thinking of something larger, of greater import, something that speaks to the gravity of your situation."

So I asked, "When's dinner and is there a dessert cart?"

Satan looked at me thoughtfully. "First of all, it's called a dessert trolley, and second, tell me what you said downstairs that has everyone thinking they're going to hell in a handbasket."

This was the moment. We were, for a brief few seconds, equals. I had something Satan wanted to hear—the ultimate question. I looked at Satan and asked, "What happens if you flunk the orientation test? Do you go to another level of hell? Are you sent back to earth?"

Satan stared at me for what seemed like an eternity. In fact, it may have been eternity. Then she said, "Damned if I know."

Our meeting lasted for hours. But let me sum up: of the 666 major things you need to know about Satan, these are the most important:

1. As noted above, Satan always takes the form of something designed to scare you. For me, it was my first wife. For others it's Arnold Schwarzenegger's maid in full daylight. But eventually you get to see Satan in his true form: six foot six, three hundred pounds, fire red skin like an old Jewish person on the beach for the first time. But without the hat, sandals, and black socks.

2. Satan is iliterate. He can't read or write. However, he's incredible at texting, where spelling doesn't matter.

3. Satan's horns are actually implants. He got them at a body-piercing studio on Melrose.

4. Satan does not have normal desires. He's completely different from anyone you'd meet on earth. He actually liked *Sex & the City 2*.

5. Many of the things we know about Satan are false. For example, Luther (that would be Martin Luther, not Luther Vandross) recommended that we enjoy music because the devil cannot stand gaiety. Not true; he just doesn't like certain types of music. The only music you're allowed to listen to in Satan's presence are Paris Hilton's album, "I Wanna Sex You Up" by Color Me Badd, and KISS tracks from the no-makeup years.

6. Satan's job is to tempt, and he knows just what each person's weakness is and how to use it. For instance, if it's Internet porn you crave, you'll be led to a windowless room with a six-foot monitor and goose-down tissues stacked to the ceiling. Then, right as you're about to log on, the only thing you'll see is . . .

Loading ⧗

You see, in hell, they don't just get you with fire and anger and torture. Sometimes it's even worse than that. It's boredom. Satan has AOL, Afterlife Online. Think about ordering *Bleached Starfish 8*, then buffering for four thousand years.

7. Satan is a fallen angel, much like Kendrys Morales. He was cast from heaven for questioning God's infallibility. In retrospect, Satan was right, Netflix *is* better than Blockbuster. And Satan, un-like the guy in the office next to you, also knew LaserDiscs would never catch on.

8. Satan has a lot of hobbies. He's a gamer. You know that guy you can never beat at World of Warcraft, the one who seems to be online twenty-four/seven? That's him, Mister I've Got All the Cheat Codes. He's a video game fanatic, which makes sense, since technically he also lives in his father's basement.

9. Satan is incredibly smart. He can explain complex things in the simplest of terms. For example, I asked him how to define the difference between art and porn. He said, "If you hang it on your wall to impress women and get laid, it's art. If you masturbate to it instead of getting laid, it's porn." Later on I asked him, "Why is the sky blue?" He said,

"When God designed the place, he felt it was too small. The decorator told him blue would make it feel more spacious." "Amazing," I said. "So do all planets have a blue sky?" "No," he answered. "It's brown around Uranus."

10. Satan is Santa for dyslexics. It is also "a Stan" for people who hate Stans. Think about that the next time your child brings home Flat Stanley.

11. Satan is a Cubs fan. This explains some of the anger.

12. Satan does not sit on your shoulder, like in the cartoons, arguing with an angel about what course of action you should take. The Master of Mayhem is much more subtle; he whispers things in your ear when you are asleep. This works especially well with air traffic controllers, who are never awake. Satan is the one who told the captain of the *Hindenburg*, "Hey, pal, it's your zeppelin, you can smoke if you want."

13. Satan invented the wrapping they use for CDs and razor blades.

14. You know the saying "Every time a bell rings, an angel gets his wings"? There's a corollary. "With every new spring blade of

grass, Satan gets a piece of ass." He is insa-
tiable. Seriously, he's tapping some new little devil fifty or sixty times a day. And always
in his favorite position—missionary.
15. The most interesting thing about Satan? He's
married. This explains the rest of the anger.

What was fascinating was that even though we had
just met, we had a connection. And a real one, not like
the kind on eHarmony where the only thing those
twenty-nine dimensions of compatibility means is that
the computer has matched up two identically superficial
people. I got the feeling that Satan liked me, or at the
minimum he was lonely . . . or that there was something
about me being an accountant that intrigued him.

Satan cleared his throat, a sound that I will never forget. It sounded like a chorus of tuberculosis patients on
a bad phlegm day. He said, "Let's get to know each other
better. Let me ask you, why do you think you're here?"

Instantly a flood of memories came rushing back.
When I was in college I got drunk one morning and
plowed into a school bus full of kids. And the worst part
was it was a school band. One of the kids needed a trom-
bonectomy.

Or was it the time I prank-called the night watchman
at the Fukushima reactor and distracted him?

Was it the time I falsely predicted the Rapture so that

half the people in Arkansas would put their possessions on eBay, where I picked them up cheap?

My life passed before my eyes. Then Tom Cruise's life passed before my eyes. I would tell you what that was like, but who needs that lawsuit? Then it was back to my life as I tried to remember every bad thing I had done.

Telling the blind person the light said "walk"?

Not being kind and not rewinding once in the 1980s?

Giving *News of the World* and Rupert Murdoch a way to hack into my office voice-mail system?

Moving copies of *Hustler* magazine into the Oprah section of the bookstore?

Even worse, moving copies of *O, The Oprah Magazine* to the adult section?

Satan's answer was "Nope. You know what it really was? It was April 21, 2004. You were in the Medical Arts Building on Wilshire. Do you remember?"

I stared in amazement. "Do you mean the time . . ."

Satan nodded. "Yep, you farted in the elevator. And blamed someone else. Do you know how many times we've heard 'He who smelt it dealt it?' Hell is full of guys like you. Why do you think it smells like this down here?"

Looking back, that gas had been pretty bad. (The night before had been "International Night" at the Shmuley household, and dinner had consisted of borscht, kimchi, and haggis.) Several people in there with me passed out, and the elevator itself dropped three floors

before recovering. Still, I didn't think that alone warranted eternal damnation.

"Level with me, Satan," I said, "an innocent cutting of the cheese isn't why I'm here, is it? What's the real reason?"

"That was the straw that broke the camel's back, but we've had our eye on you for a while." He smirked. "Look into your heart, think back. After hundreds of misdeeds in your life, the elevator incident was just the icing on the anus."

My eyes glazed over like an old man with cataracts.

Satan said, "Here, take a look at your file." In a flash a minion entered carrying a stack of file folders taller than Gary Coleman. Ironically, when he set them down, I saw it was Gary Coleman. He smiled, said, "What you talking about, Satan?" and left.

I took a cold, hard look at my life, and all the wrongs I had done while I was alive. "Was it the incident with Mr. Fredericks?" I asked. "Ha, that was a good one," Satan said and chuckled. "You were off to a nice start."

When I was a kid, Mr. Fredericks was the old man who ran the corner store in my neighborhood. He was blind in both eyes, deaf in both ears, and mute in both mouths. He was the product of first cousins who had sex on top of a nuclear test site. One day as a joke I decided to start sending him letters from a "secret admirer." The letters began innocently enough, then became more and more steamy and graphic. Eventually I arranged for this secret admirer to meet Mr. Fredericks. Using a mannequin I'd found behind a department store, I set up the unsuspecting old guy on a date. Being a nuclear mutant who'd never had a real woman, he couldn't tell the difference and fell madly in love. He began to carry the mannequin around with him wherever he went, as people snickered behind his back. They stayed together until his very last day.

"Oh, come on," I protested, "that was kind of cruel, but no one really got hurt."

"Oh, really?" Satan replied. "But there's more to it, my friend. What you don't know is that Mr. Fredericks and the mannequin consummated their relationship. And because of his nuclear-radiated sperm, he was able to impregnate her. That's right, they had a child."

"No! It can't be," I cried.

"Oh, yes. A hideous half-human, half-plastic child. And today, that child is Heidi Montag."

I was overcome with guilt. Was I really to blame for six seasons of *The Hills?*

Satan pushed on. "Think about your other shortcomings."

"My penis?"

"No! You know, character, personality stuff. Your behavior."

"Was it my driving?" I asked.

"Well, you never were the best behind the wheel," Satan said.

I guess I had been through my share of driving-related incidents. The time I throttled an old lady for taking too long in the crosswalk. The time I wiped out a family of bald eagles by drunkenly smashing my car into their tree, knocking their nest to the ground, then stepping all over the hatchlings when I stumbled out of the car.

"And don't forget the blow job while driving," Satan said.

"That was one time, and it was the only way that guy would give me a lift."

"No, you idiot, the other time."

"Hey, she was a student driver, did she want to pass or fail?"

"Guess again. . . ."

"Oh, that. Look, I'd been practicing for months trying to limber up and stretch. I could finally reach! How was I to know it'd cause a twenty-car pileup? You take your eyes off the road for one minute. You know, I can still see my teeth marks down there."

"And let's not forget, you don't exactly have a stellar track record when it comes to the holidays, either," he laughed.

I always had trouble remembering and observing the holidays. I'd spent a lifetime making last-minute excuses. When my kids had hit me up for Christmas presents, I had explained to them that we were Jewish. When they asked what we were doing for Passover, I told them I had recently converted to Buddhism. When they wanted to know the path to nirvana, I quickly told them we were now Muslim. When they asked why I was stuffing my face with bourbon-crusted pork in the middle of Ramadan, I said, "Your mother and father are pagans now."

Eventually I found it was easier to convert several times a year than to plan a family holiday.

As for forgetting our anniversary, I told my wife our marriage was technically null and void because she had slept with the preacher. Though I thought I made that up from whole cloth, it alarmed me that she didn't argue.

"You've made a mockery of religion," the devil charged, "and that's my job. And you did the same thing with the legal system. Remember?"

I had once been on the jury in a capital murder trial. The evidence was nothing more than circumstantial, and the defendant had a solid alibi and DNA evidence that put him five hundred miles from the scene of the crime. Still, that weekend it was going to be Mike Tyson versus Cicely Tyson in a celebrity boxing match on pay-per-view. Not to be missed. In a rush we found him guilty and recommended he be skinned alive, then drawn and quartered. We were so convincing that the judge allowed our precedent-setting verdict and the defendant was hauled off to meet his maker. Which is where I should be now instead of down here in hell. "Who's laughing now?" Satan asked. "Probably Cicely Tyson," I said. "Can you believe she won?"

"And of course, one of your finest moments, in the summer of 2003," Lucifer cackled.

As payback for dumping their leaves into my yard, I

had frozen my urine into homemade Popsicles and served it to the neighbors at our annual barbecue. "That's not that bad," I pleaded.

"Shmuley," he said, "you're not being honest with me. Did you forget that I see all and know all? Those weren't normal hamburger patties you served them, either. That was truly disgusting." I had been caught! How could even Satan have known about my hideous deed? What gave me away? "Most people missed it," he said smugly, "but if you looked closely and paid attention, you'd see that backyard barbecue had just a little bit extra corn."

Reflecting back on my life, I was certainly no angel. Self-copulating while driving, sentencing an innocent man to death, serving up the neighbors a poo-poo platter, these were not things to be proud of. But deep down I knew I was capable of redemption. If Casey Anthony could get acquitted, I, too, deserved a second chance. Heck, if Michael Vick could make a comeback, so could I. Besides, all I ever did was arrange one little fight between my kid's guinea pig and the hamster.

I knew somehow, someway, I could find a way out of hell and go back to earth.

Satan's Rebuttal

From the desk of Arnold Mishkin, Esq.

Dear Mr. Shmuley:

Under the New York Court of Appeals ruling in *Satan v. Plume, Blue Rider Press*, Shmuley, et al., you are required, where appropriate, to give my client, Satan, a chance to rebut or clarify any misleading and/or erroneous statements in your book so as to avoid the possibility of a libel. Forthwith, please insert this memo from my client, unedited.

Sincerely,

Arnold Mishkin
Attorney at Law
ABA-Certified Specialist
in Wills, Trusts, Divorces,
DUI, and Prenups

FROM THE DESK OF

October 2011

First of all let me say I don't remember meeting anyone named Skip. At least not anyone over ten years old. I have no recollection of any conversation with him nor do I admit he was ever in hell or that somehow he managed to escape. More important, in no event do we ever let anyone look at their file folders.

Having said that, let me take this chance to give his readers a more balanced picture of myself.

Shmuley may call it hell but to me it is another four-letter "h" word—home. Sure, it is filled with some of the most despicable people in history, but here is my point: I didn't make them. They are in God's image, not mine. So if John Wayne Gacy is in God's image, who's the bad guy? Me or the serial-killing clown in You Know Who's image?

Think of hell as a place where people come to when the Almighty Supreme Being who actually runs a very restricted country club decides they can't get into heaven. He only allows in the chosen few; me, come one, come all, come in your pants for all I care. Basically what I am saying is that God is an elitist. I am a populist.

We have no limits on who gets to stay in hell; nor do we make things difficult for our "guests." And look at our advantages: no cold winters; early dinners; no harp music. Hell is like Florida with fewer dead people.

Now let's get to me. There are so many inaccuracies I can only address the most egregious. Yeah, look it up, Shmuley, I went to Harvard, not Cornell like you, so fuck you for that snide little comment that I'm illiterate. And by the way, you spelled it wrong on page 37.

Also if I'm the sick one, how come you know what a "bleached starfish" is and I had to look it up? I don't care what porn stars say, there is no camera shot from that angle that is ever going to be attractive.

And finally . . . at least for now, you are dead wrong, I *am* happily married. Here is her picture:

The Tour: It Was the Worst of Times, It Was the Worst of Times

I must have said those words "find a way out of hell" out loud. Because in a second, Satan said, "What kind of host am I? Let me show you the rest of this place."

I figured, what the hell.

Satan's door slammed behind me and I was on my own. Satan had obviously tired of my company so I figured, why not go for a walk and see what I could see.

A few hundred yards away from Satan's Palace, I could swear I was back in Los Angeles . . . the first five shopping centers were nothing but walk-in plastic surgery clinics, medical marijuana dispensaries, and TCBY shops. Maybe this place wasn't so bad. There were some self-centered jezebels to look at, some herb to take my mind off all the rest of it, and yogurt to help the buzz. Naturally they were sold out of weed and yogurt. And the lines were thirty million deep at the plastic surgery centers. It really is L.A. except no one tries to sneak across hell's border.

Once past the shopping centers I was hobbled by a pothole in the road. A large, moving pothole with a bear trap in it. As I lay on the ground and looked up around me, it was like a scene from the Wikipedia page about Charles Dickens. There were belching smokestacks from the factories (unlike the rest of America, hell still has a solid manufacturing base). Diet soda, Crocs, enema bags, and Lunchables are all produced down there. The rough-and-tumble factory workers were just getting off their shift, and they glared as they passed me. Maybe they were annoyed by the fact that the only manual labor my hands had ever seen was compulsive masturbation, but the glares became more menacing.

Not wanting to push my luck, I ducked into an alley. A group of young toughs was huddled around a burning trash can. "We're in the middle of hell, what do you need a fire for?" I asked. As their brass knuckles speed-bagged my uvula, I began to regret our social interaction. I quickly departed the alley, removing several switchblades that had been lodged in my skull and butt cheek.

The urban decay in hell is horrible. None of the neigh-borhoods have been gentrified by trust fund hipsters.

Which would have made hell even more of a hell. In fact, I was roaming in one of the only seedy neighborhoods left without an artisan gelato shop. The food is awful. The one McDonald's in hell serves nothing but old McDLTs from the 1980s. Walking a little further down restaurant row, I came across a Soup Plantation. Upon

entering I was horrified to discover it was an actual plantation, and I was immediately put to work harvesting soup. If you've ever tried to fill a bushel basket with cream of broccoli, you know how difficult it can be. I made a break for it when the foreman went to go check on the mulligatawny section.

It was now almost five p.m. on my first day of being dead. Dusk was starting to settle and the creatures of the night were beginning to stir. Not content to write on walls, graffiti artists had taken to vandalizing passersby. It was a half hour before I realized someone had spray-painted a "Kick me" sign on my back. Although I was relieved to find people had been kicking me more out of obligation than disgust.

Suddenly a seedy guy in a leather jacket approached and tried to sell me drugs. He carried only the hardest, deadliest stuff around. Vioxx, Celebrex, Chantix, it was all there. I declined it all. "You're not a narc, are you?" he demanded. "Not me," I responded. "The only time I ever squealed was when I got a Barbie doll for my seventh birthday. She had such pretty hair." The dealer moved on in search of someone with more comprehensive health coverage.

Not wanting to be caught on the streets after dark, I checked into a nearby youth hostel. There was a group of European tourists who weren't actually condemned to hell, they were just visiting it on holiday. They could have saved airfare and just gone to Bulgaria.

When dawn broke I made a beeline back toward Satan's Palace. These streets were too rough and I wanted to be back in the relative safety of familiar ground. Even in hell, you don't want to get mixed up with the wrong people.

Everyone Is Old in Hell

As I sat down on a park bench outside Satan's Palace I started to think about my family. Where were they? They all deserved to be in hell. Especially my grandfather.

When my PopPop died, I inherited an old desk from him. Why an unemployed guy who spent WWII huffing paint in a toolshed in Omaha needed a desk is beyond me but there it was. And in the drawer of that desk was a giant stack of nude pictures of old flappers. How I loved those photos! They simultaneously got me through and brought about the end of each of my marriages. The pictures were stunning. I never knew that Fanny Brice was in that good shape. If only Streisand had looked that good naked, but only Elliot Gould, James Brolin, and every guy in New York in the '70s knows for sure.

At first I wondered why PopPop kept those around until I realized, this was how he met my grandma. Yes, there among all the other old nudes was my grandma in the flesh. She definitely looked a lot better than that one time I walked in on her in the bathroom, filing her bunions.

Was this another reason I'm in hell, the fact I rubbed one out while looking at a picture of my Bubbe?

PopPop also left behind a penknife, a collection of original Hardy Boys novels, and a membership card to something called NAMBLA. It must stand for Nice, Amicable Men Believing in Life Affirmation. (I suggest you all look it up. On your office computer. Trust me it's safe.)

All of a sudden the connection became clear. Bubbe's best friend Sylvia. Sylvia! She was the receptionist I had seen the day before. Then it dawned on me. In hell, I was meeting face-to-face with some of the dames in those photos who'd occupied so many of my waking hours on earth.

How could I have forgotten her? She was like Mary Pickford and Clara Bow rolled into one. But she hadn't looked the same. Even though she died at age twenty-seven from a gin rickey overdose, in hell she looked like

Methuselah. In fact, the only thing sexually attractive about her was she had no teeth.

It was then I realized—everyone grows old in hell. Even if you died young, soon your body turns into a tired, weather-beaten old husk. Even worse, because of the temperature, every woman has that dried-out wrinkled skin between her breasts like a fifty-two-year-old keno dealer. All that moisturizing was for naught.

When I think back to meeting those old flappers, I realize the only thing flapping was their gums and their

breasts. These women had died young and left behind a beautiful corpse, enjoyed one final time by the coroner or mortician's assistant, but then the passage into hell and time there had aged them. Everyone asks me now what my vision of hell is and I say simply this: it's a ninety-five-year-old woman dancing the Charleston in the nude, with her nipples on her knees instead of her hands.

My Return to Earth

I must have dozed off on the park bench as I was think-ing about all I had seen. In my dream I heard a voice yelling for help. The screaming got louder and louder until I was startled awake. The yelling was coming from Satan's Palace. Even though I was in hell I wanted to help. I opened the door to the palace and ran toward the sound. It was coming from the inside of Satan's Throne Room.

As I walked in I could see Larry the attendant anally impaled on his mop handle as if a rogue NYPD cop had roughed him up. He was near death, again. And coming from stall numero uno I heard the cursing.

It was Satan. "Can someone get me some goddamn

toilet paper? I've got a meeting in ten minutes and I can't go there with a bumper crop of dingleberries."

Here was my chance.

I said, "Satan, what's it worth to you?"

He said, "Shmuley? You're back?"

I said, "That's right I'm back. Didn't really think this one through, did you? God is all knowing, but you're just a Harvard know-it-all without a roll of Charmin."

He said, "For my sake, get me a roll of toilet paper, six hundred ply. It's in the cabinet."

Six hundred ply! That still has wood chips in it. Again I asked, "And in return?"

He said, "Okay, tomorrow come to my office at seven a.m. sharp and we'll talk about you returning home."

If only I had taken that Chester Karrass course advertised in every airline magazine in the world I would have been able to negotiate a better deal. But since I hadn't, I handed him the toilet paper and agreed to the morning meeting.

I walked back to my room at the motel. When I got there, the key didn't work. I went to the front desk, where the clerk explained to me that they had to release my room because they'd had a VIP check in.

I asked who.

"Ted Williams's head," he said.

Is the joke on those cryogenics people or what? They spend years setting up elaborate trusts to pay for them-

selves to be frozen for eternity only to find out that all this does is ensure they go straight to the one place where even a minus-453 liquid nitrogen–filled head will eventually melt.

The clerk was kind enough to give me a key so I could retrieve the belongings I had left in the room. When I entered, there was Ted's dead head.

The head said, "Hey, kid, I'm the greatest fucking hitter who ever lived."

I said, "I know."

He said, "Do you want an autograph?"

I immediately started to calculate how much this would be worth if I ever managed to talk Satan into letting me return to earth.

I said, "Would I ever!"

Teddy Ballgame then looked at me and said, "Then find my fucking arms."

What a total asshole. I gathered my belongings as he continued to scream at me and I left. Since there were no empty rooms at the motel I curled up next to the motel ice maker, although at these temperatures, it was more of a puddle machine.

The next morning I was at Satan's office bright and early. After an awkward moment with Sylvia the receptionist (somehow she knew what I did to her picture up on earth), I was ushered into the Big Guy's office.

Satan said, "Sit down. I appreciate what you did for me and I owe you one. What can I do for you?"

I said, "Satan, can you send me back to earth? I have so much to live for. I want to have a catch with Little Timmy and tell him he has a better arm than Ted Williams. I want to go out with the other accountants at my office and reminisce about the time we miscounted the votes so that Gwyneth Paltrow won the Oscar. I want to watch my wife grow old. Just for spite."

Satan smiled. "It's already taken care of. It's been a done deal ever since you stumped me with that question a few days ago, the one where you asked if you flunk the test in hell, do you go to hell? I had never prepared for that and now I have an answer for the next person who flunks the orientation test."

I said, "And your answer?"

Satan said, "Flunk the test and here is what happens. You take it again. That's it. Like a driver in L.A., doesn't matter how many times you crash, eventually you get your license. But Shmuley, since you made me stop and think, you go back to earth. You will be the first and only person to have come to hell and been allowed back."

I said, "What's the catch?"

Satan said, "None . . . except you need to carry out three tasks for me back on earth. If you agree, you will go back to your old life."

I said, "Name them and it's done."

He said, "First, I need you to file an extension on my taxes—I'm still looking for receipts. Second, I want you to fill in for me at a seminar scheduled for Pepperdine University in June 2011 where theologians are arguing whether there is hell. I'm scheduled to give the rebuttal to those who say there is no hell and I don't feel like showing up. Just go and tell people that there is a hell. It will be good publicity for your book."

I said, "How did you know I planned to write a book?"

Satan said, "Because I am all knowing . . . plus, you've been talking in your sleep."

I was about to ask how he knew I had been talking in my sleep, but the answer was too grotesque to imagine.

Satan then filled me in on the third task: to reveal to humanity the coming apocalypse.

Satan said, "It's part of the deal, one last chance to avoid Armageddon, yada yada yada."

I stifled my desire to tell the devil what a dick he is for saying "yada yada yada." Instead, I agreed and he handed me a piece of paper with his revelations and a warning not to open them until I was back on earth. We shook hands and then I blurted out, "How do I get back?"

Satan said, "Put on these ruby red slippers, click your heels three times, and say, 'There's no place like home.'"

This was it. A pair of ruby red slippers appeared by my feet. I easily slipped them on as they were my size and this wasn't the first time I had cross-dressed. I closed my eyes and clicked my heels three times and said, "There's no place like home, there's no place like home, there's no place like home."

When I opened my eyes a second later I was surrounded by Jesus, Muhammad, Moses, Buddha, Joseph Smith, L. Ron Hubbard, Zeus, the Great Pumpkin, that Wiccan priestess who works at the Starbucks near my house, and Satan. They were doubled over with laughter.

Satan said to Jesus, "Hey, J man, get this video on YouTube. I bet we get more hits on this than when we tricked Rebecca Black into singing 'Friday.' Now get him out of here."

Jesus approached me, laughing. He put his hand on my shoulder and, in a flash, hell melted away. I was on my way home.

The Journey Home

Ascending back to the living world wasn't as simple as I thought. It's very delicate. You can't go too fast or you get the bends. And you can't go too slow or you get the runs.

I felt myself getting lighter and lighter on my feet, until I began to float upward. I looked down and saw a sea of condemned souls staring at me with anger and envy. They gossiped among themselves, "Looks like *somebody's* sleeping with the boss."

I could tell by the way Satan watched me that he'd always remember me as the one that got away. Like that special girl in high school who pepper-sprayed you before you could even get to first base.

I continued to rise. Now it was as though I was swimming through a thick primordial fog. Hell is no place for asthmatics. It was like the smoke machine had malfunctioned at a Def Leppard reunion show. I was confused, for the Hell AccuWeather that morning had called for the usual, sunny with highs in the mid-nine-thousands.

I began to hear muffled noises. Could there be other people adrift in this fog with me? I reached out to them the only way I knew how. "Marco!" I said. "Polo!" a voice yelled. "Marco!" I responded. It went on like this for some time.

Finally we were close enough that I could make out the vague image of a man. "I'm Skip," I said.

"Herb," the silhouette replied. "Where are we?"

"I think we're in some kind of in-between world, some type of suspended animation," I answered.

"This fog is dense, but I feel like I'm slowly sinking," he said.

"Sinking? Uh . . . I'm sure you're . . . fine. Nothing to worry about. What's the last thing you remember?"

"I was on a corporate retreat in Vegas with the partners from my hedge fund. I'd brought along my mistress, posing as my wife. We were at the craps table, betting people's subprime mortgages and snorting some coke we found on a teen runaway we'd accidentally run over. Last thing I remember, I felt some chest pains and collapsed."

"Oh . . . well, I'm sure you're gonna be fine. Nothing to worry about. Hey, where'd you go?"

"Down here. What gives? Is it me or is it getting a little muggy?"

"Feels okay to me. Hey, whatever you do, try not to use the bathroom. Ever."

"Why? Use the bathroom where? Hey, is that Paris Hilton's album I hear? I love this song!"

The voice continued to drift downward, as I kept floating up. I was swimming up through the thick atmosphere. There were lights, shadows, and nebulae all around. It was like the time I mistook a tab of LSD for a Listerine breath strip. That was a rough back-to-school night.

The sights and sounds grew more intense. Images from my past flew all around me. I saw my Bubbe dancing the cancan in her prime, while my PopPop peered at her through a hole in the wall. I saw the time my father told Bill Gates he wouldn't invest in his crazy idea, that the typewriter was here to stay. I saw my wife telling the doctor, "He's a wuss when it comes to pain—better crank up the anesthesia."

Suddenly I realized how precious life was and why I needed to get back home. I needed to be there for my kids. Without me they'd go astray. My daughters would inevitably become porn stars. (That always seemed like such a good thing when it was someone else's daughters.) My boys would grow up to be distant, unable to engage, and emotionally unavailable. So they would be fine.

As the pull of life drew me closer to the surface, I was overcome with emotion. I began to hear my wife's voice—"Yes! Yes! Yes, that's it!" I began to head for the voice. I was almost home. Who else but me could teach my kids about life and love? Who else but me could teach my boys to be upstanding young men? Who else but me could really give it to my wife? But hey, who is that giving it to my wife?

It was then that I realized I was back on earth. The good news was that I was still lying right there on the operating table. Unfortunately, my wife was bent over the operating table, and one of the orderlies was right behind her. Turns out that, as usual, I wasn't the one causing her to scream like a banshee. I was coming back to life. "Hey, what are you doing? Stop that!" I mumbled as best I could. To the living it sounded like "Snnnz *rff* sht."

"Hurry, finish before he comes to!" my wife gasped. Funny, I had just traveled through an ocean of foggy soup, surrounded by ghosts, yet she was the one about to get covered in plasma.

Suddenly I felt a surge of energy. "Stop that!" I yelled and sat upright. In a rage I looked at the orderly. My face was as red as his balls were blue. "Get out!" I commanded. He grabbed some medical lubricant and a few hand towels and was out the door.

My wife cried, "Honey, you can understand, can't you? I thought you were dead. I'm sorry."

"Never mind that, you trollop, I'm back now. Back to take charge of this family, back to raise our children, back to make us whole again."

"Oh, honey!" she said, still naked from the waist down and bent over the table like a tramp. "The kids and I could never have made it without you. No matter how many sugar daddies I slept with."

She was overcome by the moment. "Honey," she said coyly, gesturing. "Let's see if that vasectomy took. Why don't you head on around back there and finish what that orderly started?"

That's my wife, always full of spunk. Usually someone else's.

I wanted to celebrate my return from death with sex so I jumped off the table and zeroed in behind her. I tried not to focus on the glowing red handprints the orderly had left on her ass. Or the fact that after his impressive manhood, she could barely feel me. Yet somehow she was excited to have me back. After just three tries, she actually yelled out the right name; it was a new record. Ninety seconds later I was asleep on the operating table again, snoring in my wife's ear and drooling down her cheek. I was back.

Hell Time

My first night back among the living, it was time for "the talk." My wife and I were sitting on the front porch after a romantic dinner at Dave & Buster's. I had won enough tickets at Skee-Ball to get her the sixteen-inch plush SpongeBob. She wanted the Hello Kitty vibrator.

She asked me about hell. I started to tell her about my three days, but she said I was only dead for three minutes. I explained to her that hell time is different. That a minute on earth is a full day in hell. She got excited; she said, "So in hell you could last during sex for two full days?"

That's when we started to talk about the elephant in the room. And I don't mean my office assistant Dolores.

She said, "Could you hear anything we were saying up here when you were down there?"

I said that I had heard everything. She did a spit take, as she often did after oral sex. "I heard you talking to the doctors about my condition. I believe your exact words were 'Do not resuscitate.' "

"I thought you weren't coming back," my wife said.

"I know. I also thought it was tacky that you changed your last name and your Facebook status," I went on. "Before the operation."

"I have to be honest," she said. "While you were gone I was with someone else."

I said, "I know, the orderly. I woke up and there you were."

She said, "No, before him; he was rebound sex after the breakup."

"I was only gone three minutes!" I yelled.

"You didn't expect me to mourn forever, did you? What about my needs?"

The truth is time is different in hell. It slows to a crawl and the more bored you become, the worse it gets. In hell, the shortest baseball game is seventy-two innings. The announcers actually tell you, "It's the bottom of the century."

Each commercial break is four hours long, and there's

no DVR. Even the conversation can slow to an unbearable pace. When people talk it sounds like Charlie Brown's teacher but without all the witty repartee.

If one could take away a lesson from this experience it would be this: you know how they tell you to enjoy every moment while you're on earth? It's because in hell there's way too many moments, and none of them are enjoyable.

Eyewitness to Hell

It wasn't until a few months after my time in hell that I decided to unburden myself and share my story. But with who? With whom? With who? That to me used to be hell—grammar choices; but now I know what real hell is. And it made me want to share my story with the "undead," as Satan calls them, those on earth who think hell is being a Clippers season ticket holder. I truly believe I was sent back to let people know, real hell is even worse.

But who to share my story with? That's when the opportunity presented itself. Little Timmy, my four-year-old, came home from Sunday school and asked, "What is hell like?" Turns out the minister had told him if he

76

didn't keep quiet about what they just did, Timmy would go to hell himself. I, of course, wanted to ask, "Keep quiet about what?—and do you need to show me on the doll where he touched you?" But since his was the question of an innocent, I decided to answer.

As I began to talk, Timmy interrupted. "Dad," he said, "let me record this on video and also as a backup on my MP3 in case we ever want to sell a book and profit off this. And maybe contact Blue Rider Press and see if we can cut a deal."

What a precocious and believable four-year-old! So,

after he grabbed his complete audio/video setup, I began to tell him about what I saw.

First I told him that when I left my body, I could look up and see him and his mom in the hospital. "Mommy was giving you Vicodin and Robitussin so she could talk to Ernani the orderly," I said.

Timmy was astounded. He said, "And just as I was falling asleep she told me Ernani might be 'a possible new daddy!' "

Timmy then asked if I had met Satan and if he had a first name. I explained to him that Satan has many names: Lucifer, Beelzebub, Prince of Darkness, Fallen Angel, Bernie Madoff, Angel of Darkness, Victor Conte, Murray Fishbein, the Serpent, the Dragon, the Leviathan, Levi Johnston, Angel of the Bottomless Pit, and Steve Bartman.

I then told Little Timmy about sitting on Satan's lap and, based on what I could see, he was clearly not Jewish. . . . I also related that in heaven Jesus is surrounded by disciples, Moses by other prophets, and Scientologists by famous actors. In hell, Satan's minions are Hitler, Bin Laden, and Notorious B.I.G. At least I think it was Biggie; it was a large man who spoke only in rhymes that made fun of Tupac.

Then Little Timmy asked, "What is the worst thing about hell?" But I couldn't bear to tell the young lad what true hell is. In hell, you wake up every night at two a.m., walk into the adjoining room, and always see the same vision: your parents having sex.

Dying and Dying Again

Spring 2011 marked a year since my hospital stay. I was still feeling some side effects. For some reason I couldn't fill out my March Madness bracket without clutching my balls. My wife found it disgusting. When I told her the other option involved *her* clutching my balls, she dropped the subject. At that point I was going through what I call "come-and-go damnation." Sometimes I had horrible flashbacks of my time in that awful inferno. Sometimes I was just depressed because my bracket fell apart in the first round of the tournament. It was like being President Obama, pre–Bin Laden raid.

On this spring morning I had to run some errands. I

needed some jock itch cream, something to reduce scar tissue, and enough beer for that day's basketball games, roughly a pony keg. I loaded up Timmy into my wife's car. It was immaculate inside. It's amazing how clean and fresh a car can seem when you're not constantly eating and farting in it. The one time when I finally bought a brand-new car, I went out and got a fart-scented air freshener just to feel at home. Meanwhile she actually had a real flower, in a little vase of water, inside the drink holder. I chucked the flower, spit my gum in the vase, and it was time to go.

As I started the ignition I was overcome by a terrible sound. My vision went blurry; my skull pounded as though it was fracturing into a million pieces. Was I headed back to hell? Then I realized it was just Barry Manilow in the CD player.

As we drove, I realized that I had a captive audience. Not "put the lotion in the basket" captive, but captive nonetheless. Good Friday wasn't far off, so I asked little Timmy, "Do you know what Good Friday is?"

"I sure do," he said, picking his nose gingerly. "That's the day Jesus died on the cross!"

"And do you know why Jesus died on the cross?"

"I sure do!" he answered in between boogers.

"Really?" I said. "And who told you?"

"I watched Mel Gibson explaining it on TMZ. He said it was because the Jews killed him."

In my mind's eye I saw Mel that fateful night, with a

bottle of Jose Cuervo on his lap, brushing past all the police checkpoints on the PCH, knocking over road signs, simplifying fancy words like "anti-Semitism" and "hate mongering" to something a child could understand: "Fucking Jews . . . the Jews are responsible for all the wars in the world."

That moment reminded me of the difference between grown-up and childlike faith. Children look to religion as a source of wonder and hope. Grown-ups use it to get out of a Breathalyzer.

Later that month, Timmy threw me for another loop. Actually two loops, if you count the time he asked what my bottle of strawberry-flavored Astroglide was for. This loop involved life or death. My wife and I have a theory: If you walk in on your spouse taking a dump, you won't be able to have sex with him or her for at least a month. Regardless of whether there's a bidet. But we also have another theory, one that involves raising kids. From the time a child first walks until about the first grade, one of the main tasks parents have is to keep their children alive. No live ammunition in the house. Don't approach the ice cream man if his van has no doors, no windows, and a driver with no teeth. Don't let him go to work as a mule for the Mexican cartel.

Little Timmy was almost ready for kindergarten, and there was still one thing he couldn't grasp (besides his junk when he was peeing). He couldn't grasp that when a human body meets a moving car, bad things happen, and any footage of it will end up on those snuff sites based in the Netherlands.

One day Little Timmy and I had stopped at Sweden Crème for a snack. Sweden Crème is the kind of small-town place that sounds like an erotic massage parlor but, sadly, just sells ice cream. Every town has one. McCook has Bone & Jerry's, Benklemen has 69 Flavors, and in Holyoke, they've got Blew Bunny and Good Hummer.

I bought Little Timmy a huge cone, because, as a parent, I just love when my kid is bouncing off the walls till four a.m. on a sugar high. Timmy took the cone and, faster than you can say "childhood diabetes," he was flying out the door and across the parking lot, headed right for the street.

"Timmy, stop!" I yelled.

He stopped and I jogged to catch up to him. Then I stopped to catch my breath. God, I was out of shape. Gasping for air, I wheezed, "Son, you can't do that!"

Just then I saw a little pile of fur in the middle of the street. I seized the moment to teach him a lesson. I pointed to it. "See that? That's a hairpiece from that old guy who was run down last week. He had shrunk so much in his old age that the driver didn't see him. And he just kept going. The cops still haven't caught the guy."

Timmy gazed quizzically at the ratty old hairpiece blowing up and down. "Was it Mel Gibson who was driving, Daddy?"

"I don't know, son," I said. "I just don't know."

Why I Decided to Share This Story: The Coming Events

The real reason I'm back here was not as I had hoped—to spend time with my kids. The real reason I was allowed to return is to carry out Satan's third task and act as a prophet here on earth. I'm here to share with humanity what I've seen and tell them about what the future will bring. I am here to warn the world about the coming events. I am here to scream from the mountaintops like a yodeler being sodomized by a yeti.

In Colton Burpo's book, he referenced the coming war that will destroy the earth. Jesus and the angels will come and they will fight the legions of Satan in a battle that will end life as we know it. Some interpret this as

Armageddon. Others interpret this as the divorce between Arnold and Maria. As someone who's been to hell, I am privy to a different future for mankind. Much as there are the seven seals that will be broken, there are seven revelations to tell you about. But please, don't try to make a hero out of me. I don't have the sophisticated training of Harold Camping, who predicted the end of the earth on May 21, 2011, then postponed it till October 21. I'm merely a messenger, sent to earth because Satan's AOL was down.

I hate to paint such a bleak picture but, to be honest, there's no hope. No amount of praying to whatever god you believe in can save mankind. Sorry to be a downer but the future is more hopeless than Andy Dick's acting career.

The Revelations

The coming chaos. The beginning of the end will come when Apple goes bankrupt and everyone is forced to go back to their PC. This causes a crisis as the Windows operating system will be too incomprehensible to those addicted to the streamlined technological crack that are our Apple products. Within weeks there will be anarchy in the street, dogs mating with cats. As always in a time of crisis, people will turn to a new leader. John Hodgman.

The coming of the Antichrist. In 2013, in an effort to curry favor with young people, the Senate will lower the voting age to twelve. The effects of this catastrophic decision manifest themselves almost immediately. Narrowly defeated by Obama at the start of his third term, winner of the video game primary Mike "The Situation" Sorrentino becomes a revolutionary youth leader and brings us one step closer to the end. His 501c GTL camps create a small army of youth-interest voters, aged twelve to seventeen, nicknamed the "Leatherbacks" due to their scorched skin from time in the tanning chambers. Fast-forward to the year 2024, when he throws his support behind the rising GOP female star . . . I have two words for you: President Octomom.

The coming bankruptcy. What plunges us into hell isn't the subprime mortgage crisis, and it isn't the Chinese. It's the response of the World Bank to an e-mail from Nigeria. Thinking they've found a way to double their limited resources, they reply to a message from a billionaire named Mr. Prince Dakumbo. Within twenty-four hours, no one in the entire world has any money in their accounts except for three guys in a corrugated tin shack in Lagos who promptly spend all the cash on chips, dip, and seven-thousand-dollar racing stripes and shiny spinning rims for their five-hundred-dollar jeep.

The coming disaster. It's a given that Al Gore is one of the smartest men who ever lived. He invented the

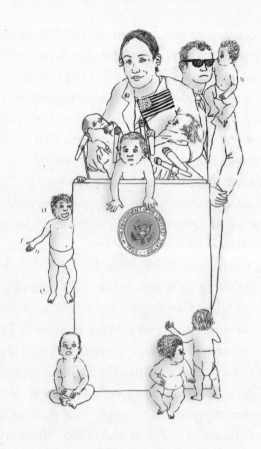

Internet, as well as a cable channel watched by as many as a dozen people at once. But his inability to admit a mistake will cost us. It turns out that long ago he hit a wrong key and we should have been worrying about global *worming*. It turns out the world will end much like the movie *Tremors*. With Kevin Bacon as our only hope. And with all those night crawlers, President Octomom's solution is "more fishing." More fishing leads to a depletion of our oceans. Which leads to a food shortage, which leads to . . .

http://www.washingtonpost.com/national/discovery-of-worms-from-hell-deep-beneath-earths-surface-raises-new-questions/2011/05/31/AGnzJTGH_story.html

The coming famine. In 1840 the population of Ireland was nearly wiped out by a potato famine. In 2040, the population of America will be wiped out by a potato chip famine. Forced to give up their junk-food diet and for the first time confront green, leafy vegetables, Americans will be thrown into a tailspin. The craving for junk food will lead to the invention of things such as beer-battered spinach. The only people able to cope with the new thirty-calorie-a-day diet will be the Olsen twins, Lara Flynn Boyle, and Mischa Barton.

The not coming coming. By the year 2020, men will be so addicted to Cialis, Levitra, and Viagra that they will be unable to reproduce without the aid of medication or a hot tub. Much as we've lost the ability to run like our ancestors, we will lose the ability to procreate. Since natural sildenafil is found in the Middle East, this means EDPEC, a cabal of Middle East nations, will control our sex lives. It's bad enough they're screwing us on oil; soon they'll be screwing us on screwing.

The coming Rapture. On Judgment Day at the precise moment, the heavens will open and the earth will tremble. As the ground begins to crack, revealing the gates of hell, only a chosen few will be levitated into heaven. Actually, a chosen few seven billion people. But the 144,000 who think they are going to be taken away in the Rapture will go straight to hell.

The Most Important Facts About Hell

The most important thing to know about hell is also the worst thing about it: in hell, Satan kills you over and over and over again just for his own amusement. It would seem the one and only upside to being in hell is that at least you've got the dying part over with, but they won't even let you have that. Turns out, hell is ironic. Which sounds like that Alanis Morissette song. Which ironically is hell to listen to.

So down there, every day ends with you dying, only to be brought back again to start the whole thing over. Here are but a few of the ways they go about it. . . .

Heart attack. Just like here on earth, heart attacks are one of the biggest killers in hell. Especially of men. But it's never the good kind of heart attack. Not the kind that's the result of eating your weight in jelly donuts, followed by a thirty-six-hour coke binge, culminating in a three-way with Marilyn Monroe and Elizabeth Taylor (both down there, by the way—the Jewish God doesn't like converts). In hell what triggers a massive coronary are mandatory Pilates and spinning classes.

Mauled to death by a snarling pack of Navy SEAL war dogs (Osama bin Laden only). Your disembodied leg is then dry-humped by a basset hound that couldn't quite make the squad.

Dying of embarrassment. In hell, you can literally die of embarrassment as Satan's entire army of demons gathers around to laugh at old photos of you from awkward stages of your life. Your young face full of braces and headgear; in a leisure suit about to attend a key party; the hair metal years; that time you joined Greenpeace just to impress a girl; the mullet years; that one month you tried to dress like a rapper; awkward facial hair; and of course the camera phone footage you took of yourself in a dress.

By the way, in hell, whatever you died of is considered a preexisting condition. This guarantees that no insurance company will cover you. You'll spend fifteen to twenty years on hold with your health care provider, trying to talk to a live person. Then your call will drop. As a result, whatever your condition is it will slowly deteriorate, lead to other, worse conditions, and eventually leave you a shut-in and an invalid. Once the poor circulation, festering bedsores, and early-onset diabetes have set in, you'll die a slow death sitting in a rotten Barcalounger in a pool of your own filth. Probably the same thing that killed you on earth.

Shooting spree. Everyone is disgruntled in hell. Ten thousand millennia of white-hot flames blistering the crack of your ass will do that to you. People are ready to snap at any moment. Especially on the job. The last thing you want to do at work is move somebody's cheese. The number of workplace shootings in hell averages twenty-five per day. Almost as high as the U.S. Postal Service. Most people work in Hell's Kitchen. It's a nice enough area as long as you stay clear of the Jets and Sharks. A lot of people are happy just to be employed, but if there's that one guy that everyone knows is about to lose it, try to get on his good side. Grab him a slice of cake next time there's an office birthday. Or try one of those "The worst day fishing is better than the best day working" bumper stickers. And if he does get that pink slip and comes back with an AK-47, well, it doesn't really matter. You'll just wake up and start all over again tomorrow. There are no sick days in hell.

Little-Known Facts About Hell

💀 Hell has a national park. Unlike California, hell can actually afford to keep its parks open. And a lot of people like to visit them. There are some beautiful rock formations, including the Devil's Punchbowl. Sadly, every visit to a national park ends with being eaten by a large grizzly bear.

💀 The pitchfork was not Satan's first weapon of choice. For several hundred years, he reigned in hell toting around a gigantic spork.

💀 In the throes of a midlife crisis, Satan once bought himself a brand-new Corvette with the license plate "Say 10." He was going to paint flames on the sides, but decided that would look stupid.

Satan's favorite holiday is Halloween. Not because of ghosts and evil spirits. The week after Halloween, all the candy corn that no one ate gets shipped directly to hell.

Even Satan cannot get a steak cooked rare in hell.

Satan and his minions have rigged the last six seasons of *American Idol.* How else do you explain Taylor Hicks?

Satan is now the second-largest U.S. debt holder, behind China. He's buying up thousands of foreclosed properties and will combine them to start a giant amusement park, Standing-in-Line World.

When Satan was first cast out of heaven and fell all the way down into hell, he faked a broken leg and tried to sue.

Satan is in the gym a lot. And he's one of those guys that constantly checks himself out as he pumps iron. Afterward he has a big meal of nothing but lean protein. Usually a couple of arms and a torso.

Satan loves celebrity gossip. He follows the triumphs and the heartbreaks of Jennifer Aniston incessantly. Even now, he secretly hopes she'll find some way to get back together with Brad. Through all her highs and lows, she perseveres. If you are in fact sent to hell, you'll be expected to discuss this for hours on end. And woe be to the man who calls her Jennifer No-Man-iston.

- Hell has never frozen over. (Conversely, Mrs. Shmuley has never thawed out.)

- Sometimes things do arrive in hell inside a hand-basket. They include, but are not limited to: Guns N' Roses, the U.S. economy, Lindsay Lohan's career, the VCR, Donald Trump's presidential campaign, and that fixer-upper house you just bought. Which leads to the other riddle that would stump even Satan. What the fuck is a handbasket?

- The road to hell is not, in fact, paved with good intentions. It was paved by nonunion laborers and is now riddled with potholes. Also, the convenience stores along the way have a terrible selection and no bathrooms. So you probably want to hold on to the bottle once you finish the Gatorade.

- Hell doth have a fury like a woman scorned. Come on, what kind of expression is that? Really? An eternity of being stabbed in the neck with a flaming pitchfork, or your girlfriend causing a scene at the Cheesecake Factory? The worst she can do is destroy some of your stuff. And if it really does get that crazy, the sex was probably so good it was worth it.

- "Satan" is just his first name. His full name is Satan Bartholomew Beelzebub Higgenbottom

Demonseed. Although you never hear that unless he's being yelled at by his mother, Ann Coulter. His name also used to have several umlauts over it, but he dropped them, claiming they were "too ethnic."

- Hell has to get its water pumped in from elsewhere. Where do you think your toilet leads? Naturally the tap water is filthy in hell, so most people buy the store brand, Pitchfork Springs. Although even in hell, you now get dirty looks for not having a reusable water bottle.

- Hell has a visitors' day, when loved ones from back on earth can come see you. Security has tightened in recent years, ever since they caught a guy trying to keister in a cell phone. Families get a chance to catch up, but the conversations get a little repetitive. "How's things back on earth? You doing okay? How's that family of five I brutally butchered . . . oh, right."

- Hell has a smoking section.

- There is no hard alcohol in hell. The flames would cause every drink to light up like a novelty party shot at a sorority girl's twenty-first birthday. Drinks are watery. This has cramped the style of many an international jewel thief who's been sent down there. It's hard to look debonair with a Smirnoff Ice Pineapple martini.

🐲 Recreation isn't quite as much fun in hell. The most popular game down there is Beer Kong. The player throws a Ping-Pong ball into a small plastic cup of beer. If he misses, he is chased down by a large gorilla and ripped to shreds.

🐲 Anyone who ever robbed a convenience store is sent to hell and forced to live on a diet of Budweiser Cheladas, Hostess fruit pies, Charleston Chew, and grape-flavored cigarillos. Amazingly, no one has mentioned to Satan that this is better than people eat back on earth.

🐲 There's always hubbub about his influence on earth, but the only country Satan exerts a direct hand in is Finland.

🐲 If you thought you knew where Taco Bell's meat substitute comes from, guess again.

🐲 Hell is full of the Amish. And Satan *loves* electricity.

🐲 The largest dildo factory in history is located in hell. Believe me when I say you don't want to know why.[1]

---

1. It's outrageous. The largest dildo factory used to be in Connecticut. Martha Stewart ran it. In 2009 she claimed her company was too big to fail, got a bailout from TARP, paid herself a bonus, and moved the entire operation to hell because of the nonunion labor and Satan's tax breaks. It was there or India, and hell has less dysentery.

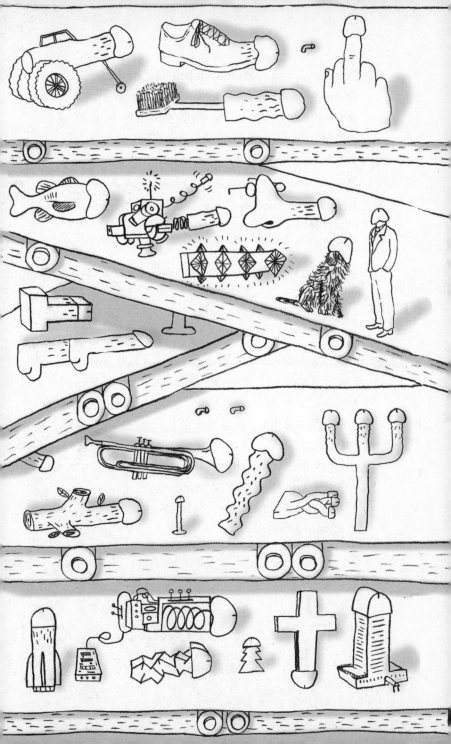

😈 You see a lot of celebrities in hell, but all the interesting ones go to heaven. Turns out Jesus likes a good story. Hell has Mister Rogers and Mother Teresa. Heaven gets Hunter S. Thompson.

😈 Everyone down there got sexted by Anthony Weiner.

😈 In hell, your mother-in-law still makes you go to church every Sunday even though you're already in hell.

😈 You always have to use a condom, and it always breaks.

😈 In hell, even the semiattractive women all have cats.

😈 An actual snowball, sitting there in hell, lasted longer than Mel Gibson's *The Beaver* did at a theater near you.

😈 Other things that a snowball in hell has outlasted:

- Gary Busey's attention span
- Newt Gingrich's 2012 campaign
- Any given generation of the iPod
- *Parker Spitzer*

Things to Do in hell

If you know where to look, there's a lot of fun things to do in hell. Hopefully this chapter will act as a handy guidebook to some of the entertaining ways to spend eternity while rotting away.

There's actually quite a bit of nature to be seen down in hell. You can walk the nature trails at Brimstone National Park. They have a famous geyser there, Old Miserable, that goes off exactly once every seven hundred years. But although the timing is consistent, the location is not. Old Miserable makes sure to blast its rocket of scalding-hot water out exactly wherever you are standing. Doesn't matter where, if you're in the park, it'll find you like a hungry bear finds the slowest kid in a family of hill-billies; it'll find you like a tornado finds a trailer park. The three-foot-wide gusher will shoot you a hundred feet in the air like a supercharged enema. Think of a searing-hot bidet—that's Old Miserable. But the good news is it should finally dislodge that last piece of porterhouse from your intestinal walls. If Elvis had stood over it he might still be alive. And by the way, for all you conspiracy buffs, Elvis is indeed dead, in hell and "all shook up."

Most of God's creatures are pure of heart and go straight to heaven, so there aren't a lot of animals at Brimstone National Park. Among the only animals that do get sent to hell on a regular basis are those yappy little dogs that get shuttled around in designer handbags here on earth. The more expensive the handbag, the more tor-turous the little mongrel's existence will be in the after-life. A teacup Chihuahua that spends its life snapping at strangers from a fifteen-thousand-dollar Hermès bag will promptly be placed in a blender, liquefied, and given to Satan's cat as a digestive.

Like to work out? They have a gym in hell. Stay away from the locker room, though, as it's entirely populated by old men with eighteen-inch scrotums who refuse to wear a towel. When they sit on the toilet, you finally learn the meaning of the word "splashdown." And the men's ex-ercise room is no picnic, either. There are plenty of great classes, Hot Yoga, Hot Kickboxing, Hot Spinning, and the

Hot Coal Fire Walk Treadmill. I tried to work out there once, but unfortunately, every single machine is covered in the last guy's sweat. And the bench press had skid marks.

There's plenty of shopping in hell. Hundreds of wonderful boutiques and furniture stores. Unfortunately they're only for the guys. For women, there's a heavyweight championship fight every night followed by six hours of video games. Ladies, should you ever go shopping with a guy in hell, you will be mortified as he proceeds to tell you that every single pair of jeans does in fact make your ass look fat.

Big sports fan? You can always drop in to one of hell's local sports bars to catch a game. Sadly, most of the TVs only show Asian amateur jai alai and major league soccer.

In hell, one can live out every depraved fantasy one has ever dreamed of. No scenario is off-limits, but it comes at a price. It's always just a little bit off. While I was in hell I asked for a night of unbridled sex with Jessica Alba. Instead, I was given the Duchess of Alba. . . .

(Actual photo. Believe it or not, this isn't Lucifer.)

Although I can assure you that what she lacks in facial beauty, she more than makes up for in penis size. Think Lady Gaga in the year 2070.

Enjoy fine dining? You're in the wrong place. Hell's food court has the most stomach-churning slop you've ever had to choke down. Orange Judas, Hell Pollo Loco, Church's Chicken. Interestingly, the only dessert they serve is angel food cake. But they spit in it.

Deep in hell's wine country, you'll find the one nice restaurant, the French Lavatory. The dining is exquisite— ten Michelin stars and a thumbs-up from Bridgestone. Unfortunately the clientele is made up of insufferable foodies who insist on hearing more about how the cow they're about to eat, "Sidney," was raised. After a ninety-minute spiel on its upbringing and education you'll be craving the lava rocks and rotten toad meat back at the mess hall.

Eternity with Morrie

Even though there are plenty of things to do in hell, the one thing I craved when I was there was human companionship, someone to talk to who understood me like a schizophrenic understands Glenn Beck.

Because in hell, as on earth, companionship in life is something we all look for. Some people find it in family, some people rent it by the hour.

The people around you can be role models. Having a mentor to help guide you through adversity is invaluable. Without my father's guidance, how else would I have ever learned about the STD lemon juice test?

And as far as friends, when I was among the living,

I had plenty of compatriots from whom I could seek advice. Like Gus, the old wino with tuberculosis who lived in the alley behind my office. He taught me how you can subsist on a diet of nothing but Chivas Regal and Bit-O-Honey. Or Chantilly, the hooker with a heart of gold, who worked the streets near my favorite burger stand. She never talked too much, though; she was afraid her pimp would slice off one of her fingers for wasting time. Also, more often than not, there was a penis in her mouth. Usually mine.

So in hell I sought out a new peer group. People I could relate to and discuss shared experiences with. Someone to watch my back, so as to avoid the constant anal raping by winged, fire-breathing demons.

It was around then that I met Morrie. Morrie was a kindly old man. Back in the early 1900s, he'd worked as a handyman in Margaret Sanger's first Planned Parenthood clinic. He was doomed to hell after his lax safety standards led to over fifty women electrocuting themselves to death in what is known in feminist circles as the invention of "retroactive birth control." He wasn't like most of the other people I met down in hell. For one thing, he enjoyed the rectal pillaging from those fire-breathing demons. But more important, he had a tranquil, sagacious air to him that radiated wisdom. (To be fair, in a world made entirely of molten lava, everyone radiates.) I took to having hourly chats with Morrie as we sauntered through the doomsday wasteland. Our relationship could be characterized as mentor-protégé or convict–prison bitch.

"Morrie," I said to him one day as an incubus went to town on his colon, "to be honest, there's probably a few old friends of mine who've ended up down here. Maybe I should try to find them."

"Bad idea," he said. "Let me guess, these are people you haven't seen in years, decades even, who you kept in touch with online? Don't go looking for your Facebook friends in hell. They didn't want to meet face-to-face in real life; they sure don't want to do it here. Besides, the only social network anyone uses down here is Ashley Madison." Morrie gazed into the distance, I scratched my chin, and the incubus climaxed, rolled over, and lit a cigarette.

Another time, I bumped into Morrie right as he was about to duck into a peep show. I didn't realize that was his cup of tea. He told me when he worked at the vibrator factory, he used to go all the time to do market research. Of course, we were still on the gold standard back then. Consequently, several strippers were accidentally killed onstage after being pelted with doubloons.

"Morrie, do you think it's possible to find true love in hell?" I asked him.

"No way," he replied. "Everyone's got an ulterior motive in this rotten place. I met a woman here once that I really fell for. She had a body that just wouldn't quit—except for that time she dropped dead from an aneurism. I thought we had a real connection. Turns out she just thought of me as a piece of meat."

"Morrie," I said, "you have the body of a seventy-seven-year-old man who's been decaying in hell for almost a century."

"I know, she was sent down here for cannibalism. She wasn't dating me, she was dry-aging me."

One day I decided to join Morrie on one of his trips to go mall walking. I met him early in the morning at the Gates of Fire Galleria. He tightened up the Velcro on his Rockports and we were off. Morrie said he originally tried listening to music during his mall walks, but in hell all they give you is a Zune that holds four songs.

"Morrie," I said as we walked quickly past a Hellshire Farms kiosk, "I feel like we've really become good friends. Do you think we'll stay in touch if one of us ever gets out of this place?"

"Of course not, you idiot. I've already filled out my paperwork. If I ever get out of here, I'm getting reincarnated as a toilet seat in a ladies' room."

"Wait, you mean people can sometimes be reincarnated?" I asked.

"Yeah, but the waiting list is backed up for a couple millennia. You can speed things up, though, if you're willing to sleep with the right people."

"Really? Have you tried it?"

"What do you think this demon on top of me is doing?"

Eventually my dear friend Morrie was granted his voyeuristic reincarnation fantasy. He came back to earth as a toilet seat, where day after day unsuspecting women would plop their bare behinds down upon him in a never-ending procession. Unfortunately it was in the ladies' room at Club Bounce, the nightclub for BBWs and the men who love them.

Before he went back, Morrie taught me a few other life lessons.

- Your family is always your family. Even down in hell they'll still be with you. Close to you. Which isn't as great as it sounds. Most of the family members who get sent down here are those overly touchy uncles.
- Mall walking is useless if you stop at the food court on every lap.
- The Zune really is a piece of shit.
- Respect your elders; listen and learn from them. No one else is going to. Most of the ones down here died of neglect.

- Old men's ears and noses continue to grow, even in the afterlife.
- Life is not a sprint; it's more like a marathon. You start out confident and strong. By the very end you're wheezing, gasping for air, and crapping yourself.

Most Interesting People You'll Meet in Hell

Morrie wasn't the only famous person I met in hell. Over the course of my three days, I not only ran into a lot of historical figures and fascinating faces, but there was also a "reservations" section, similar to ones they use at Hertz rent-a-car, with a list of celebrities who were yet to arrive. I don't mean to frighten anyone, but I took a cell phone picture of the board and, with a few questions to the clerk (Oscar again), found out why they were going to hell.

Mitch Albom. The good news, he gets to spend a whole lot more time with Morrie.

LeBron James. Won't LeBron be surprised when he finds out God is from Cleveland?

Jon Gosselin. Although in hell they'll try their best to evict him once they realize he's worthless, contributes nothing to their society, and refuses to get a job.

Everyone who ever worked on Wall Street. Except, oddly, Bernie Madoff. If televangelists can con their way into heaven, why can't he?

Senator Lindsey Graham. You know why. Your staff knows why. Even your mom knows why. It's okay, we don't care. But Satan and God are both pro gay rights and hate hypocrites.

The Kardashian sisters. Well, just the ugly ones.

Lady Gaga. She was actually destined to get into heaven. But she showed up to the pearly gates in her own modern interpretive angel costume that she said "reinvented the whole afterlife thing." Jesus finally got to use that new trapdoor he'd installed.

George Hamilton. It's his chance to get a really great tan.

Tom Brady. You just can't have three Super Bowl rings, knock up a supermodel, leave her for another supermodel, and still have everyone love and adore you as an American hero. You just can't. It's too much. It's not right.

Kanye West. Got really, really close to heaven but the vanity thing got him. Also, he kept interrupting Saint Peter.

Any Winehouse's hairdresser. Not Amy, just the person who talked her into that beehive. No wonder she overdosed.

Rick Santorum. It turns out God created man-on-dog sex. And is really mad you are against it.

Antonio, the Saturday morning waiter at Morels in the Palazzo in Vegas. He is so slow, if he'd run Schindler's list, we'd all be dead. He was last seen telling Lucifer, "I'll show you what an eternity is."

Pau Gasol. For committing the sin of sloth (did you watch that series against the Mavs?) and for not even bothering to add the fourth letter to his first name.

Tim Tebow. God will tell him, "You know what? Go try your Little Mr. Perfect act somewhere else." On the plus side, in hell at least he'll get some playing time.

David Schwimmer. But good news, Schwimmer, they have dinner theater in hell.

Anyone who's ever played Angry Birds.

Burt Reynolds's toupee. Burt gets heaven. But God will say, "I made everything in the universe except that. It looks like a squirrel mated with a Brillo pad."

Nicolas Cage. He had been guaranteed entrance to heaven after *Raising Arizona*. By the time he did *The Weather Man* there was to be at least a little purgatory. But *Drive Angry* sealed his fate. Sadly, down in hell, even Medusa asks him, "What's the deal with your hair?"

Satan's Favorite Jokes

Think of the worst comedy club you've ever been to. Now think of the worst comic there. That's Satan, who appears every night at the Chuckle House in the Hell Airport Marriott. And here are his favorite jokes:

A Scotsman, an Englishman, and an Irishman are sitting in a bar in hell, reminiscing about home. "Back in me pub in Glasgow," brags the Scotsman, "fer every four pints of stout I order, they give me one fer free!" "In me pub in London," says the Englishman, "I pay fer two pints o' Guinness and they give me a third one free!"

113

"That's nuthin'," says the Irishman. "In my pub back in Dublin, you walk up to the bar, they give the first pint fer free, the second pint fer free, the third pint fer free—and then they take you upstairs and you have sex for free!" "Is that true?" asks the Scotsman. "Has that really happened to you?" "Well, no," says the Irishman, "but it happens to me sister all the time!"

~

A guy is stuck down in hell, talking to Satan. He starts rambling on about how lousy a wife he had back on earth, until Satan finally says, "You know, I don't understand what you're complaining about. All the other guys in here only have compliments about your wife."

~

An E-flat gets sent down to hell. Satan says, "Sorry, we don't take minors."

~

A woman walks into hell with a duck under her arm. Satan asks, "Where'd you get the pig?"

She says, "That's not a pig, it's a duck."

Satan says, "I was talking to the duck."

~

Did you know that heaven and hell are actually right next to each other? They are separated by a big chain-link fence. Well, one day hell was having a big party and it got a little out of hand. God heard the ruckus and arrived to find his fence completely smashed by the wild partyers. He called the devil over and said, "Look, Satan, you have to rebuild this fence."

Satan agreed. The next day God noticed that the devil had completely rebuilt the fence . . . but it was two feet farther into heaven than before.

"Satan!" God beckoned. "You have to take that fence down and put it back where it belongs!"

"Yeah? What if I don't?" replied the devil.

"I'll sue you if I have to," answered God.

"Sure," laughed Satan. "Where are you going to find a lawyer?"

~

A guy is sent down to hell and Satan asks him, "Why is the front of your pants all bloody?"

The guy answers miserably, "My wife caught me with another woman and cut off my penis."

"Oh, come on," replies Satan.

The guy says, "If you don't believe me, I'll show you." He proceeds to rifle through his suitcase and pulls out this long thin thing and hands it to Satan.

Satan bends down and looks closely and says, "Why, this is just a cigar."

The guy looks puzzled and says, "I have it here somewhere," and proceeds to fumble through his pockets and comes up with another long thin thing, hands it over, and says, "See that?"

Satan inspects it closely and says, "You asshole, that's just another cigar."

Now the guy staggers backward and steadies himself, leaning on the wall, and says, "Son of a bitch, I must have smoked it!"

~

A guy went to use the bathroom in hell. He was in there for a while, yelling, so one of Satan's minions went to check on him.

"What are you screaming about?" the minion demanded.

"Every time I try to flush the toilet something keeps biting my balls!"

"Well, for starters, try getting off the mop bucket."

~

Bill Clinton is in hell. When he gets there the devil greets him and offers him three ways to spend eternity. They go to the first door and the devil shows him Rick Perry hanging from the ceiling with fire under him. Bill says, "Oh, no! That's not how I want to spend all eternity!" They go to the second door. The devil shows him Rush Limbaugh chained to the wall, being tortured. Bill says, "Oh, no! Not for me!" They go to the third door. Behind it is Ken Starr, chained to the wall, with Monica Lewinsky on her knees giving him a blow job. Bill thinks and decides, "Hmm, looks okay to me. I'll take it." The devil then says, "Good. Hey, Monica, you've been replaced."

Ways to Ensure You're Going to Hell

Turns out there are only three things that get you automatic passage to hell. Everything else is subjective and Satan makes case-by-case decisions, but if you have done any of these three, it's straight down.

1. Botoxing your eight-year-old.
2. Being a member of the Westboro Baptist Church.
3. Pretending your nine-year-old went to heaven and profiting off his fake story. (Oh—and one other thing—if you are Jennifer Petkov and you taunted a terminally ill seven-year-old girl on Facebook, Satan can't wait.)

Things Worse than Hell

It's important for everyone here on earth to note that although hell is bad, there are things on earth worse than hell:

- Internet cat videos. How many times can I watch a kitten crash headlong into a sliding glass door?

- Yelp and Citysearch. Everyone's a critic. Someone sinks their life savings into their lifelong dream of opening a restaurant, only to get crucified online by a college kid who accidentally got cilantro on his chicken curry.

- Running out of hot water in the shower before you're done masturbating.

- Having to attend your kid's elementary school graduation . . . or even worse, your nephew's.

- Square dancing.

- Sex with Hugh Hefner.

- Nonprofit work.

Epilogue

ell really changed my life.

Like opera, German cooking, and prison sex, it's not for everyone. But for one Skip Shmuley, I am not now who I was.

For one thing, while writing this book, I lost my job with the accounting firm. They said I was taking too much time trying to warn the world of the coming apocalypse and not spending enough time on my bean counting. That, plus the missing petty cash. Plus what HR affectionately called the "Christmas party zipper incident."

But it didn't matter because I had already decided to quit and devote myself to my new interests. . . .

Like tinkering with my inventions. In fact, I came up with a great one that everyone should have in case they ever end up in Satan's Throne Room. I call it 20,000,000 Flushes. And trust me, you'll need more than one.

Like lobbying Congress to outlaw vasectomies. Who cares about the growing anticircumcision movement? Why are men allowing themselves to be routinely browbeaten into undergoing a dangerous, painful, and in my case temporarily fatal operation just so their wives or girlfriends can go off the pill? My friend, when she suggests the vasectomy, remind her why God gave her a mouth to open and a nose simultaneously to breathe with.

And finally, I've devoted myself to kids. Not my own, of course, but other people's kids, foster kids, dozens of them. Do you realize what you can make off these future little criminals?

There is a fortune in government money to be made if you don't give in to their incessant whining and waste it on food, clothing, and shelter.

So that's my story. It's as real and true as the Burpo family story or the other true, factual, not-made-up stories of everyone who has ever gone to heaven and come back.

Because make no mistake—there is a heaven and there

is a hell. I've been to one and hope to go to the other. And if there is one thing I am sure of in this life, it's that where you end up does not depend on whether you believe in Jesus, Allah, or the Book of Moses . . . it is solely, one hundred percent dependent on whether you fart in an elevator.

A Final Word from Satan

FROM THE DESK OF

To: **Mankind**
From: **Me**
Re: **This dopey book**

First of all an apology for letting this schmuck return to earth. It would have been so much easier just to send you all a tweet with my warnings of

125

what lies in store for the wicked. Truthfully I could have summed it up in less than 140 characters.

Here's the tweet. "Most of you are screwed."

But call me compassionate; I thought hearing from Skip would have made my warnings seem more real so at least you could prepare. That's the last time I send a putz to do the work of a tweet . . . as opposed to tweeting my putz.

Anyway, the main point of me having the final word, besides the fact that I get ninety-five percent of Shmuley's royalties under our deal if I write something, is that I wanted to let you know that I hate anyone who spends half their day worried about "going green."

Is there anything stupider than that? There's a great idea, Al Gore. Go fight pollution by flying a private jet around the globe burning up a thousand years' worth of oxygen, to give a speech telling people to recycle a plastic bottle that gets picked up in a non-smog-checked truck, driven three hundred miles to a coal-powered recycling plant, then cleaned and shipped back so the process can start again. Idiots. It's why there's hell. It's for people who recycle and are smug about it. And it's also for people who fart like Shmuley. So we're talking ninety-five percent of New York City.

Bottom line: Shmuley is only half right. True, I hate people with digestive problems. But I really hate people who have holier-than-thou smug attitudes about recycling. And if you are in an elevator bragging about your Prius and the great sustainable organic shrimp you ate last night and you rip a bad one, you might as well just get ready to burn forever.

But for all my complaints about Shmuley, and despite him painting a pretty inaccurate picture of me personally, his depiction of death and what happens postmortem and what you see in hell is one hundred percent on the money. For thousands of years man has speculated on what happens after death. Some say you go to a core place where you see Barry (that's what I call God; his actual name is Barry Fishbein); others say that since time doesn't truly exist, death is just a reboot for all probabilities; still others say your brain and body simply cease functioning and there is just eternal nothingness.

Nope. Shmuley gets it. A few of you go to heaven, and the other seven billion are going to be spending a lot of time with me. And arriving here soon. Just not in a handbasket. Whatever that is. And whatever a handbasket actually is, I hope it causes global warming.

So I look forward to our meeting. After all, I'll be seeing most of you soon enough. As for Skip, I have a message for him in the form of an old Irish blessing:

May the road rise up to meet you, especially if you get run over like that old guy who only left a ratty old hairpiece behind.

May the wind always break in some other guy's elevator.

May the sun shine warm upon your face, aging you prematurely yet still making you look younger than those ancient flappers.

And until we meet again, may your wife reluctantly hold your swollen botched vasectomy testicles in the palm of her hand.

All my best,

Satan

So that's it. . . .